D1156841

HOW HOT A MANAGER ARE YOU?

ERNEST DICHTER, Ph.D.

Chairman of the Board
Ernest Dichter Motivations, Inc.

Professor of Marketing
Long Island University School of
Business and Mercy College

MCGRAW-HILL BOOK COMPANY

New York   St. Louis   San Francisco   Auckland   Bogotá
Hamburg   London   Madrid   Mexico
Milan   Montreal   New Delhi   Panama
Paris   São Paulo   Singapore
Sydney   Tokyo   Toronto

Library of Congress Cataloging-in-Publication Data

Dichter, Ernest.
  How hot a manager are you?

  Includes index.
  1. Psychology, Industrial.   2. Management.
I. Title.
HF5548.8.D49   1987   658.4   86-10356
ISBN 0-07-016782-6

  234567890   DOC/DOC   893210987

ISBN 0-07-016782-6

The editors for this book were William A. Sabin and Barbara B. Toniolo,
the designer was Naomi Auerbach, and the production supervisor
was Teresa F. Leaden. It was set in Baskerville
by Braun-Brumfield, Inc.

Printed and bound by R. R. Donnelley & Sons Company.

*Dedicated to my wife, who has been a top manager
of my business and my life*

CONTENTS

PREFACE

Managing is a euphemism for guiding others, getting things done, giving and executing orders. Political dictators, presidents, and super-visors are all managers. Basically, people who achieve preset goals manage at least themselves.

Philosophies, people, and objects comprise three types of managerial problems. In each case we assume that we can influence the objective world, other people, and ourselves (often at the same time). It is a grand illusion. Yet without management of some sort, we would let ourselves be guided by Kismet—by fate. In fact, many cultures and indeed whole societies are based on such passive convictions. More often than not, they include willful faith in such powerful forces as mantra, multiple gods, and one almighty deity.

The author, and presumably the reader, believes that it is possible to influence others and bring significant change to the world in which we live. Determination is the key. Without it, some people would opt for luck or predestination, which may be only a clever way to float on the currents of life, letting accidents of minor and major proportions govern their paths. On the other hand, people who are determined to fight back—to resist, to wrest control from the forces that be—will learn to use psychotechniques of mastering inner and outer resources. In other words, they opt for *management.*

Managers, particularly top managers, are often isolated. Belief in the future, in progress, and in the ability to grow or adapt will be their gratification. Challenge is the forte of top managers. They plan, make decisions, communicate. They act as guides or teammates. Their emotions are kept under strict control. Above all, managers must be innovative and creative while accepting luck and help from others as manna from heaven.

Management is not a one-way street. It does not simply consist of barking orders and expecting them to be faithfully carried out. Coworkers should be thought of not as subordinates but as partners. A wise manager understands that people reach their greatest potential when they are motivated to grow and develop. The manager's success depends on respect—both given and received.

At times, every manager is called on to play the role of psychologist, friend, and adviser. Understanding the why and how of human motivations can lead to managerial success. Finding out why people behave as they do and, more important, how to influence and motivate them to behave in a desired fashion can give an astute manager invaluable leverage. But the manager who does not know how to translate these findings to everyday behavior has only created hollow promises.

Real motivations are not always apparent. Why do many of us want to wear fashionable clothes or look youthful? What does a person want out of life? Forty-five years of experience have taught us to dig deeper. Customary psychological tests are too often transparent. Would you ask applicants for a sales position whether they liked people? If applicants wanted the job, they would easily guess the right answer. We are searching for truth—truth that will permit us to make suggestions and offer practical remedies.

Putting every aspiring top manager on the psychoanalyst's couch for a couple of years might produce deep meaningful insights. It would be wonderful to offer a miracle pill—wash it down with water and become a top manager in 10 minutes (a cheap trick). This book is somewhere in the middle. It requires some work on the reader's part. Then again, it may have more realistic, lasting influence than dazzling but superficial stage effects.

Everyone needs a plan. *How Hot a Manager Are You?* also has a plan. The book is divided into seven chapters. Each deals with an important function of management.

1. Decision making
2. Planning
3. Creativity
4. Emotions
5. Motivation
6. Teamwork
7. Communication

Each of these functions is important for top management. We have devised so-called projective tests for each of these abilities—*projective* meaning there is not always a right or wrong answer. Nor should you kid yourself about your real qualifications. The more honest the answers, the more valuable the tests will be for you. Try to project yourself into the various situations and analyze what your actual response would be.

Certainly, we would hope you are not tempted to select a more ethical or moral answer simply to place yourself in a better light. If you are honest with yourself, you can request the same from your colleagues. At the end of each section, you will find many practical recommendations to strengthen your performance as a top manager.

The clarity and effectiveness of most of the tests have been assessed by administering them to managers on various levels.

ACKNOWLEDGMENTS

I want to express my thanks to Jeanine Babcock, my assistant, for contributing many ideas and supervising and typing the manuscript. I appreciate the patience and help I received from William A. Sabin and Barbara B. Toniolo. Their criticism and contributions were vital.

DECISION MAKING
THE MOST IMPORTANT JOB FOR A HOT MANAGER

WHAT IS YOUR REAL MANAGEMENT STYLE?

Decisions and risks are closely related. If the alternatives and their potential results are clear, there is no decision—no choice—to be made. It is obvious which is the better (or only) alternative.

In the life of a company or, for that matter, in people's personal lives, there are many choices to be made. If the goal is clear, there is no problem. No questions even need to be asked. If lowering the price of merchandise is almost certain to increase sales, little managerial skill is needed to figure out what to do. As uncertainties increase, decisions become more complex. Then the style of decision making is put to the test.

Every time you make a decision, to some extent you play God. That is the thrill, the gamble—trying to anticipate tomorrow morning's headlines. Of course, there are many case histories where a top manager plunged into a dubious situation. Perhaps the manager was tired or felt there was no rational way of deciding.

Subconscious factors also affect decision making. You may lean ever so slightly toward one alternative because you like or dislike the person involved. It is important to know your coworker's decision-making pattern—as well as your own.

Management patterns can be altered through training and behavior modification. Often it is best to find a position suited to your style of operating. Just as you have a lifestyle, you also display a particular decision-making style. The following test can help you evaluate your management style. We tried to hide any obvious answers. There are no correct or incorrect answers. Give it a try, and we'll discuss the results later.

┌─ **Test** ───┐

Select the one answer for each question that best expresses your feelings.

1. You are a managing director. Sales of your company have been falling quite drastically. The analysis of this decline has yielded contradictory results. Several explanations and solutions have been offered. Which are you most likely to accept?
   - (*a*) One particular territory has been responsible for this drop in sales. They should be alright in other areas. ☐
   - (*b*) The sales manager in this area has not been performing satisfactorily and should be fired. ☐
   - (*c*) Something is wrong with the product line. It should be changed. ☐
   - (*d*) Employee morale should be improved by offering incentives and promotions. ☐
   - (*e*) Let's wait and see. This negative trend may reverse itself soon. ☐

2. Things are going well. You are ahead of the competition, and your colleagues are happy. What are your plans for the future?
   - (*a*) Leave well enough alone. ☐
   - (*b*) Determine the reason for your success, and refine the method (procedure). ☐
   - (*c*) Look for further progressive ideas. ☐
   - (*d*) Promote the person(s) responsible for the success. ☐

3. Out of nowhere, a new brand of merchandise—in direct competition with yours—appears on the market, and its sales take off. What is your strategy?
   - (*a*) I appeal to customer loyalty, emphasize product superiority, and wait for the storm to blow over. ☐
   - (*b*) I discuss the situation with my associates and find out why this situation occurred and what can be done. ☐
   - (*c*) I develop an improved product without finding out why the competitor made inroads in this market. ☐
   - (*d*) I order a systematic study made of the market (the reason for my failure, etc.). Then I choose a plan of action. ☐

4. Prices had to be increased for one line of merchandise. It was a gamble. Contrary to expectation, the public has resisted the increase, and it now appears that prices will have to be reduced to retain the market. How was your original decision to increase prices reached?
   - (*a*) I involved the whole group and collected opinions. ☐

└──┘

(b) I decided alone. After all, I'm the manager. ☐
(c) I warned everyone that it wouldn't work but went along with the group. ☐
(d) I expressed my opposition strongly. When my prediction came true, I said "I told you so." ☐

5. In a meeting when I have to decide which steps to take to remedy a situation, I
(a) Wait until all the participants have had their say and then side with the majority. ☐
(b) Try to cut through the hesitations. I use my clout to get everyone to reach a decision. ☐
(c) Ask all the participants to put their arguments on slips of paper, then go along with the majority, even if I disagree. ☐
(d) Sleep on an important decision and ask others to do the same. We meet a few days later to arrive at a decision. ☐

Put your test answers aside for the moment while we review three managerial styles of rational decision making.

Speculative Managers.   In these uncertain times and in the next few years, a plethora of speculative managers will surface. Since many facts needed for evaluation will not be available, speculative managers must jump into the partial or often complete unknown. They justify this pattern of behavior as the wisest in periods of uncertainty, and they call this approach *belief in growth* or *positive thinking* rather than by its real name: *taking chances*.

Timid Managers.   At the other extreme are managers who act only when very little can go wrong. Whether it be a merger, an addition of a product line, or the hiring of personnel, timid managers are likely to accumulate all the facts first. Timid managers are afraid to make wrong decisions and act only when all possibilities of risk have been removed.

"I want to be able to sleep nights," say the timid decision makers. Although they lack the courage to jump into the stream of things, they will amost never admit it.

Straddlers.   Only when positive and negative results are evened out will straddlers venture a decision. They've got one leg on either side of the fence. They consider themselves wise. After all, they will be held responsible for the losses. With any luck they might make the company some money. They can quote anyone—from Moses to Ben Franklin—that it is best to balance good and bad.

There are many examples of decision-making patterns which lead to success. Difficulties arise when managers superimpose their own styles in direct conflict with others in the company. Even more problems arise if there is an ongoing internal struggle. And when something does go wrong, who is blamed? A subordinate? The devil?

Whether in business or politics, *decision making* is probably the most important job of a manager. Now pull out those test answers and see how you score.

Scoring and Interpretation*

The following answers designate you as a speculative manager:
1. (*a*), (*c*), (*d*)   2. (*b*), (*c*), (*d*)   3. (*b*), (*c*)   4. (*a*), (*b*), (*d*)   5. (*b*)

You are a timid manager if your answers involve the following points:
1. (*a*)   2. (*a*)   3. (*a*)   4. (*a*)   5. (*d*)

The straddler is characterized by answers such as
1. (*b*)   2. (*a*)   3. (*d*)   4. (*c*)   5. (*a*), (*c*)

*The scoring is the result of both pretesting and commonly expressed attitudes of various types of managers.

Management is characterized by a myriad of styles. Today, speculation is considered extremely important and can take the credit for the excellent performance ratings of many modern companies. A real entrepreneur or top manager must show a certain degree of progressive thinking and defend speculation—even if risk is involved.

By its very description, timidity is seen as cowardice. To make it sound better, we'll translate it as caution.

The straddler is probably the wisest of the three—if she or he doesn't tarry too long on the fence. The U.S. automotive industry suffered major losses to the Japanese by waiting too long before entering the compact car market. Then meeting the competition was costly indeed.

If your answers were mixed, you could interpret your management style as a blend of the three. The preponderance of one type of answer clearly indicates your inclinations as a manager.

"THAT'S FINAL!"—HOW OFTEN DO YOU SAY IT?

People in a restaurant sometimes reveal how sure they are of themselves by their behavior. Often, a person will call the server back again and again to change the order. In business, it is considered prudent to "sleep" on an important decision. Yet, many managers believe in being guided by intuition.

In this test, we are less interested in *what* choice you made than in *how* you made it. Did you take your time deciding? Did the problem stick with you afterward, or did you forget it immediately?

The options you select can reveal to you your own qualities as a decision maker. Approach each series of choices with an open mind, and observe *how* you go about making up your mind. If you want the test to be effective, you *must* project yourself into each suggested situation as though it were really happening to you. Of course, it would help to have all the data on hand, but that is not always possible. Even in everyday situations, you can never be certain that some important element has not been overlooked.

Test

Select the one answer for each question that best expresses your feelings.

1. You have to make a rapid choice among three new fashions for your spring collection. Which would you pick?
   (a) A very chic, ultramodern dress that might not sell well but will help the image of the store. ☐
   (b) A modern one that is obviously out to impress. ☐
   (c) A conservative, quietly elegant outfit. ☐

2. You need an assistant for your journalistic work. Which type of person would you hire?
   (a) Bright, quick, but unsystematic. ☐
   (b) Competitive, creative, interested in moving ahead. ☐
   (c) Very reliable, carries tasks through independently, but seldom generates original ideas. ☐

3. How would you decorate your office?
   (a) Unusual design, colors, and furniture. ☐
   (b) To complement my personality; if I were small, then with small patterns; if I were exuberant, then with big designs, etc. ☐
   (c) Functional, modern, in good taste. ☐

4. You have just met three new employees. Whom would you invite to lunch first?

(Continued)

(a) The warm, shy, timid person. ☐
(b) The person not tied to traditional roles. ☐
(c) The strong, self-assured, successful person. ☐

5. You have been offered three new jobs. Which one would you take?
(a) One offering freedom and great challenge but not much security. ☐
(b) One that is steady, secure, and quite interesting. ☐
(c) One that provides a chance to work with a great teacher. ☐

6. You have earned a $4000 bonus. On what would you spend your money?
(a) New car. ☐
(b) Unusual vacation. ☐
(c) Fancy new apartment. ☐

Scoring and Interpretation

To help you know what kind of decision maker you really are, we tricked you a bit. We are not as interested in the specific decisions as in *how* you made them. Now, go back to each choice and fill in the following information on Chart 1 which follows on page 7. Remember, treat each decision as if it were a real one.

1. In the column entitled "Time," write the time it took you to decide, in minutes or seconds.

2. In the next column, check to what degree you weighed the pros and cons.

3. Now check your mood *after* deciding, from very relaxed to very tense.

4. Next record how sure you are of your choice: are you certain, or do you still have doubts?

5. In the rightmost column, assess your reaction to being told that you should have chosen otherwise, that is, your decision was wrong. Would you be angry, defensive, ready to stick with it, or open to reconsidering?

Add the scores in each column and divide by 6. The result is your average score for each column.

On the decision-making profile chart (Chart 2, top of page 8) mark the average score for each column with a dot or cross on the vertical line. Connect the dots. The graph that results will give you an interesting decision-making profile of yourself.

There are no "good" or "bad" answers. If you are careful in making

(Continued)

CHART 1

DECISION	Time	How was decision made?	How did you feel about it after?	How sure are you?	Is your mind made up?
	Actual time to make decision (minutes or seconds)	Very impulsive — 1 Somewhat impulsive — 2 In between — 3 Somewhat deliberate — 4 Very deliberate — 5 *(Score)*	Very relaxed — 1 Somewhat relaxed — 2 Balanced — 3 Somewhat tense — 4 Very tense — 5 *(Score)*	Very definite — 1 Somewhat definite — 2 In between — 3 Somewhat indefinite — 4 Very indefinite — 5 *(Score)*	Will reconsider — 1 May reconsider — 2 Casual consideration — 3 Probably stick to decision — 4 Definitely stick to decision — 5 *(Score)*
1					
2					
3					
4					
5					
6					

CHART 2

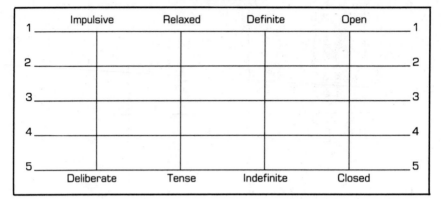

decisions, you may fare better in general, particularly if you can defend your choice.

If you take a long time to reach a decision, but then decide impulsively simply because you cannot, or did not, want to weigh the alternatives calmly—or if you have doubts afterward— training in more deliberate decision making may help you to avoid mistakes.

DO YOU DECIDE WITH YOUR HEAD OR WITH YOUR HEART?

Decision making is rarely a purely sober and rational procedure. Matters of the heart—emotions and deep psychological factors—invariably creep in to influence our decisions. Elaborate systems have been developed, now with the help of computers, to aid the executive and leader in the decision-making process. "What if" software can give answers to questions that help to weigh the pros and cons and the risks involved.

How do you decide—with your head or with your heart? Take the following test, and then let's talk about it.

─ **Test** ─

Select the one answer for each question that best expresses your feelings.

1. You are engaged in the manufacture of quality baked goods. A soft-drink company specializing in a new process of making juice is

for sale, and it can be acquired for a relatively small investment. Which of these options reflects your point of view?

(a) Since both companies are in the gourmet field, I could add considerable revenue to my company without great expenditure. ☐

(b) I have serious doubts whether soft drinks are of any interest to me or to any of my associates. ☐

(c) I could hire a soft-drink expert to inform me of the ins and outs of acquiring the company. ☐

(d) I feel I am being unfaithful to my present company by spending my time thinking about another company. ☐

2. One of your associates is enmeshed in one personal problem after another. This employee has excellent qualities but cannot avoid this proclivity for disaster which often affects the quality of work. Something must be done.

(a) This is a business, not a psychotherapy clinic; I'll have to let this employee go. ☐

(b) If the associate straightens out, we might have a valuable member on our team. I'll suggest counseling. ☐

(c) I'll set a time limit, and if the employee shapes up, I'll let this pass. ☐

(d) Perhaps our environment caused the problem; I'll let the employee go but give a high recommendation. ☐

3. Your department has bought some equipment. After the fact, you find that you overpaid, or rather that the person in charge of purchasing did. You are calling the person to task for the mistake. Which of these explanations are you most likely to accept?

(a) The salesperson was really down and out. I wanted to help with an order. ☐

(b) I am sorry. I'll pay for the difference out of my own pocket. ☐

(c) I thought it really was a better grade of merchandise. ☐

(d) I am convinced we'll get better service than from the manufacturer who sells for less. ☐

4. The wife of one of your best customers likes a special pattern of dishware. It does not pay for your company to continue this pattern. What do you do?

(a) I inform this client that I can't keep this pattern in stock any longer, simply for his wife. ☐

(b) I realize that it would break her heart not to be able to replace her pieces with this pattern, so I make it specially for her, regardless of the cost. ☐

(c) I write off the costs for the manufacture of this pattern as promotion costs. ☐

(d) I ask the customer to pay for the extra expense involved. ☐

(Continued)

5. One of your associates had a serious operation, and now this employee is less valuable to the company since he or she can neither spend long hours in the office nor travel. What do you do?
   (a) I find easier work and keep the employee on. ☐
   (b) Reluctantly, I let the person go. ☐
   (c) I offer a pension and early retirement. ☐
   (d) I keep this person on staff as a morale booster to other employees. ☐

Scoring and Interpretation

1.	$(a) = 1$	2.	$(a) = 1$	3.	$(a) = 4$	4.	$(a) = 1$	5.	$(a) = 3$
	$(b) = 2$		$(b) = 4$		$(b) = 1$		$(b) = 4$		$(b) = 1$
	$(c) = 3$		$(c) = 3$		$(c) = 2$		$(c) = 3$		$(c) = 2$
	$(d) = 4$		$(d) = 2$		$(d) = 3$		$(d) = 2$		$(d) = 4$

Compute your scores according to the values given in the above key.

A score of 16 to 20 shows that you decide more often with your heart.

A score of 5 to 8 puts you in the other extreme—those who decide with their heads. The rational decision dominates in your case.

A score of 9 to 15 shows that you vary with the problem. In our group of about 100 top managers, item 1(a) was the most frequent rational decision (60 percent). On the other hand, when a human being was involved, as in item 2, (b) was checked in 40 percent of the cases and only 1.6 percent checked the most sober decision—(a).

In item 3 (c), 40 percent decided rationally; in item 5, (a) was chosen by 50 percent of the respondents.

In other words, once a human being is involved, the heart seems to take over.

In a study for Detroit, we found that Americans wanted small cars as early as 1965. The top manager in charge of the decision to switch to compact cars did not want to believe this visible trend. Furthermore, he declared that this market should be opened up by the foreign competition and then when the market was ripe, the U.S. manufacturer would jump in. We know what happened.

His dislike of compact cars seriously interfered with his decision-making process. Consumers' feelings were not taken into consideration either. He made the wrong decision because his heart overpowered his rational thought process.

Top managers must be careful. Innermost feelings, which are sometimes completely subconscious, should be taken into account in decision equations. Figures, observations, and goals are frequently manipulated to conform with our secret wishes—often without our even realizing or admitting it.

When you are confronted with complex alternatives, make sure you have considered fears, wishful thinking, and hoped-for results in your decisions.

But how do you know when to let your emotions rule? Certainly, when the destiny of a coworker is concerned, it is good to know that even top managers listen to their hearts. Yet an emotional decision-making approach can be dangerous when the success of a company is at stake.

Greater consideration for people's well-being does create staff loyalty, for the image of the company is certainly more human—from both within and without. And so it should be. Isn't the corporation just an association of people working together? If employees are happy, if they know their destiny is considered important in corporate decisions, they will be more likely to cooperate with management and, in the final run, they will produce more.

SAYING YES TOO EASILY CAN BE COSTLY

Are you guilty of saying yes too easily? Test yourself first, then let's talk.

┌─ **Test** ───

Select the one answer for each question that best expresses your feelings.

1. You are asked to go overseas to fill a vacant post as a manager of your company's branch. Good working conditions and promotions are included. What is your reaction?
   (*a*) I have to consult with my family, friends, and/or relatives. ☐
   (*b*) I would rather decline. It means too much upheaval. ☐
   (*c*) Yes, of course, I'll go. It sounds like an excellent opportunity. ☐
   (*d*) It all depends on the circumstances. I'll think about it. ☐

2. Thinking back to the last 2 years and remembering some of your decisions, how many of them would you make differently now?
   (*a*) 1 to 3 ☐
   (*b*) 4 to 8 ☐
   (*c*) 9 to 12 ☐
   (*d*) 13 or more ☐

(Continued)

3. If you or your associates had known the consequences, which one of these various decisions would have been made differently?
   (a) Hired different people. ☐
   (b) Not have merged with another company. ☐
   (c) Not have lent money to certain clients. ☐
   (d) Carried different merchandise. ☐

4. What would you be most likely to do before making a decision?
   (a) Act intuitively and fast. ☐
   (b) Always sleep on my decisions. ☐
   (c) Map out in my mind or on paper all possible consequences. ☐
   (d) Discuss all the possibilities with my associates and close friends. ☐

Scoring and Interpretation

1.	$(a) = 2$	2.	$(a) = 4$	3.	$(a) = 1$	4.	$(a) = 1$
	$(b) = 4$		$(b) = 3$		$(b) = 2$		$(b) = 3$
	$(c) = 1$		$(c) = 2$		$(c) = 4$		$(c) = 4$
	$(d) = 3$		$(d) = 1$		$(d) = 3$		$(d) = 2$

Compute your scores according to the values given in the above key.

The higher the score, the less inclined you are to say yes too easily. The highest score is 16. The lowest is 4.

Having checked those answers which indicate your readiness to make rapid decisions can put you in the group scoring from 12 to 16.

The middle group scored 8 to 11. We have graded item 3 according to the importance of the decision. Not lending money to clients received a 4 since it might result in clear losses.

A score of 4 to 7 puts you in the camp of those people who act too quickly.

"If only I had known." All too often managers do not consider all possible consequences, and they say yes too quickly. Saying yes is easy but sometimes costly. Cutting through the Gordian knot may seem like a sign of decisiveness but can indicate a lack of self-discipline instead.

Think about the consequences. Anticipating the results (whether it's accepting an invitation for a speech or introducing a new product) can help forestall embarrassment or future problems. Visualizing the real situation—the weeks, months, and years after the word *yes* has been so easily used—can avert many complications and difficulties. A modern manager should systematically record all possible consequences before reaching a decision.

In a French movie that appeared a few years ago, a man consents to be married although he has vowed to remain a bachelor. The bride stands at the altar, beautiful in frilly white lace. She fiddles with his tie. He wheels around and flees the church, suddenly and dramatically aware of his impending loss of freedom. The audience cheers his courage. How many decisions would you rescind, if you could?

When legal matters are involved, such as lending money or expanding credit, the lender should be aware of the possibility that the client may declare bankruptcy, using usury as a defense. In a way, whenever you make rapid decisions, you should consider that you become a partner with the person in whose favor you decide.

Thinking about a decision first and then sleeping on it can have the simple but valuable result of revealing alternatives in a different light. Imagining the decision as having been made can also avoid wrong and rash decisions. So "Let me think about it" is usually a wise attitude.

WHAT IS YOUR PROCRASTINATION SCORE?

In Mexico, they call it *mañana*—I'll do it tomorrow. *Procrastination*—is it a disease? A bad habit? A game? It may not be threatening enough to call in a psychoanalyst, yet sometimes we wish we had not delayed. At other times, we are glad we did.

Which type of procrastinator are you? Take the test; let's find out.

┌─ Test ──────────────────────────────

Select the one answer for each question that best expresses your feelings.

1. You have finally finished a report which was long overdue. How do you feel?
   (*a*) What was the fuss all about?   ☐
   (*b*) Hallelujah!   ☐
   (*c*) I wish I had not acted so quickly.   ☐
   (*d*) I am just waiting for the next crisis.   ☐

2. A good friend tells you the real reasons you postpone actions and decisions.
   (*a*) I enjoy being the center of attention.   ☐
   (*b*) I am really afraid of tackling the problem.   ☐
   (*c*) I could change, if I really wanted to.   ☐
   (*d*) I secretly hope someone else will take care of the problem.   ☐

(Continued)

3. You have to make preparations. Which of these chores will make you feel most guilty if you postpone it?
   (a) Financial report. ☐
   (b) Vacation preparations. ☐
   (c) Calling a board meeting. ☐
   (d) Firing an employee. ☐

4. How are you most likely to feel after you have finally done what you were supposed to do?
   (a) Somewhat let down. ☐
   (b) Elated. ☐
   (c) Next time, I will not wait. ☐
   (d) I probably will delay next time, too. ☐

5. There are different procrastination types—Some people like to have a clear desk and no unfinished tasks, others feel a clean desk is a sign of compulsion. Check the answer you most agree with.
   (a) I know that this is so from my own observation. ☐
   (b) True, but I can't let this trait govern my activities. ☐
   (c) With some effort I can change my personality considerably. ☐
   (d) This is a lot of baloney. Postponing things is just a bad habit. ☐

6. You have a continuous battle with a colleague. No matter how much time you allow, the job is always completed a few days late. This tardiness disrupts the whole department. Which explanation are you most likely to accept?
   (a) I can do only so many things. I had to decide which comes first. ☐
   (b) I guess I was afraid of tackling the job. ☐
   (c) You are absolutely right. I will really try to be on time from now on. ☐
   (d) What's the big deal? A small delay won't make any difference as long as the job gets done. ☐

Scoring and Interpretation

1. $(a) = 2$	2. $(a) = 3$	3. $(a) = 4$	4. $(a) = 1$	5. $(a) = 4$
$(b) = 3$	$(b) = 2$	$(b) = 2$	$(b) = 3$	$(b) = 3$
$(c) = 4$	$(c) = 1$	$(c) = 3$	$(c) = 2$	$(c) = 2$
$(d) = 1$	$(d) = 4$	$(d) = 1$	$(d) = 4$	$(d) = 1$

6. $(a) = 3$
   $(b) = 2$
   $(c) = 1$
   $(d) = 4$

Compute your scores according to the values given in the above key.

A score of 18 to 24 classifies you as a procrastinator who uses different rationalizations and excuses.

A score of 12 to 17 can be the result of various combinations. Item 2(c) elicited 60 percent of the answers from our pretest panel.

In item 3(a), 40 percent felt most guilty about postponing the preparation of a financial report.

In item 4(c), 50 percent agreed that next time they would not wait.

Taken together, we see a pattern of remorse emerging.

A score of 6 to 11 describes procrastinators who need a real boost or help.

Procrastination is another form of decision making, albeit a negative one. Postponement, fearing consequences, and not making up your mind leave all possibilities open. If you cannot decide, you delay, hoping things will be decided through accident or other external forces.

Understanding the true reasons for pushing things aside provides many answers on how to circumvent the procrastination process. Even the worst procrastinators will get things done when they have to.

In a study on charity donations, we found that withholding the contribution until the last moment provided some people with an extra value. They were being wooed and they loved the attention. Once they had sent the money, they were forgotten. Reassuring potential donors with words and deeds of continued attention works wonders.

If you have chronic procrastinators on your staff, they may simply crave attention. Freud might call them *anal*—they hold on as long as possible. Assuring them of continued attention and providing them with other forms of rewards often help them over the hurdle.

As farfetched as it may seem, delay in toilet training may lead to procrastination. Once I have done my duty, so to speak, mommy will lose interest in me and so will my supervisor!

Another type of procrastinator is the person who waits for the magician, the therapist, the guru to appear. If the wall seems too high, you sit down and wait, hoping secretly that it will crumble or someone will offer you a psychological crutch to get over it.

No one delays all tasks. Some of us rush headlong into life as though it were a bowl of cereal and pluck out all the raisins. Then we nibble away at the cornflakes one by one, in no rush whatsoever. Or we push the bowl aside, cover it with our napkin, and try to forget about it altogether.

Often the reason for delay is that the tasks are considered difficult or unpleasant. But knowing the reason for procrastinating is half the battle. Usually procrastinators react adversely to being controlled by events. The pleasure of being in the driver's seat is a positive inducement. Managers, in particular, like to be in control. And is this any wonder?

Warnings and threats of dire consequences usually are not effective with procrastinators. After all, they are not operating on a rational level. Instead, providing help or teaching procrastinators to break their assignments into smaller tasks that can be handled more easily usually works quite well.

Procrastination Therapy

The time you are saving by delaying is usually lost later in some other way, for instance, by having to correct or repeat a task. Most of us learned of Julius Caesar's dilemma about whether to cross the Rubicon. He eliminated further hesitation by crossing and stated, "*Alea jacta est*" (the die is cast).

Here are some suggested therapies for overcoming procrastination:

1. *Jump in and worry later.*   This is a radical, but effective, form of cutting short the deliberation. It's the old sink-or-swim philosophy, but it works.

2. *Set a goal and inform your friends or associates of these dead-lines.*   Additional pressure is helpful in getting you to work.

3. *Seduce yourself into starting a task.*   "Just look," says the Moroccan carpet salesperson, "Take off your shoes and feel its softness." It's the talk-yourself-into-it routine.

4. *Fantasize.*   Finish the assignment in your dreams. Imagine the satisfaction—the deserved celebration—when the task is complete.

5. *Switch the logical order.*   Instead of starting at the beginning, start in the middle. Turn things upside down.

6. *Make a game of it.*   Rather than consider an assignment as a heavy task, make it into a puzzle to be solved, a riddle to be answered. Modern schools use this method for learning with excellent results.

Without delay, turn the page and go forward. Now that you know all about procrastination, you don't need it any longer.

ARE YOUR WORK HABITS THE REAL BOSS?

You are about to hire somebody. You have checked the qualifications, but you may have overlooked one of the most important factors: work habits. Does this person work better alone or with others? Can this person wait for results, or does he or she need them instantly? This chapter may help you become more aware of people around you, how they work, and what work situation is best suited to them. Test yourself.

┌─ Test ─────────────────────────────────────

Select the one answer for each question that best expresses your feelings.

1. On the wall of a colleague's office is a sign: "I do it myself." What is your reaction?
   (a) This is my kind of person, because I feel that way also. ☐
   (b) What arrogance! ☐
   (c) This appears to be a proud person. I wonder whether she or he would accept help. ☐
   (d) Usually, doing it myself is the fastest way. ☐

2. You have been part of a very successful project. What makes you feel most proud?
   (a) My ideas were on the right track. I worked out most of the solutions myself. ☐
   (b) I learned a lot from my colleagues and made many friends. ☐
   (c) We all solved the problems jointly. It was a wonderful team. ☐
   (d) We had patience. ☐

3. If you were a musician, what would you see yourself as?
   (a) Conductor. ☐
   (b) Member of a trio or quartet. ☐
   (c) Member of a great orchestra. ☐
   (d) Soloist. ☐

4. You are admiring the pyramids or a great work of architecture. What are you most likely to be thinking about while looking at the object?
   (a) What a great architect and engineer designed this project! ☐
   (b) This engineer knew how to organize the work and got the cooperation of coworkers. ☐
   (c) Imagine how many people must have labored on this job to get it accomplished! ☐
   (d) How many years it took to accomplish this task! ☐

5. You are given an assignment to set up a schedule for efficient operation of a commuter train, to remodel a house, or to reorganize the advertising department of your office. What do you do first?
   (a) I lock myself in an office or workroom and think the whole project through. Then I assign the tasks. ☐

(Continued)

(b) I call together possible collaborators and ask them to contribute their ideas and meet with me afterwards. ☐

(c) I organize the job in various specialties and skills and make one person responsible for each particular area. ☐

Scoring and Interpretation

1. (a) = 2   2. (a) = 1   3. (a) = 2   4. (a) = 1   5. (a) = 1
   (b) = 3   (b) = 3   (b) = 3   (b) = 3   (b) = 2
   (c) = 4   (c) = 4   (c) = 4   (c) = 4   (c) = 3
   (d) = 1   (d) = 2   (d) = 1   (d) = 2

Compute your scores according to the values given in the above key.

In our pretest we found that most people agreed with the cooperative answers such as 1(c): 2(b) or 2(c); 4(c); and 5(b).

The only exceptions were items 3(a) (28 percent) and 4(a) (31 percent).

Here the single achievement was more admired, although in the case of the pyramids 33 percent checked item 4(c), emphasizing the cooperation needed.

In solving an assignment in item 5, 66 percent checked (c).

A long time ago in a book, part fantasy, part truth, an experimental farm was described as the center for personal therapy and work training. Visitors were asked to record everything they expected from their lives and work. Then a psychologist analyzed their positive and negative work habits. Some were visually oriented, others were tactile, and still others were motivated by their olfactory sense. Additional differences were being able to think in abstract terms and preferring to have things made concrete.

But the most important factors were the *preference for working alone* or in a group and the *need to see immediate results*.

We selected these two factors for our tests since they can help you better understand your own work habits and, even more importantly, prevent wrong assignments for your staff. Knowing how you work best can make a big difference in choosing the occupation or role within an organization that is right for you. Many tasks are more efficiently performed by people who prefer to work by themselves. Other assignments cannot be accomplished unless a group effort is involved.

Some are loners. Loners are convinced that they can do most things better than others, and they feel uncomfortable about having to share their successes or failures.

Partnerships frequently split up because people cannot work together. One partner or another may feel that sharing the credit (or blame) for a job means a personal loss.

If you work with another person, usually the two of you can produce better results in half the time. The credit due is then twice what it would have been for one person working alone, and there is enough for both.

Most of us feel that working together benefits us, or we wouldn't get married, form associations, or start partnerships. But we need to learn more about cooperating with others. Even a concert soloist must depend on others: the audience, music critic, press agents, stagehands, etc.

By fitting our special talents in with those of others, we can arrange projects in such a way that each person realizes the benefits. The greatest rewards, including personal prestige and achievement, generally come from interacting closely and efficiently with others.

Thus, cooperation is becoming more accepted as a tenet of modern management theory. Although it is contrary to the Western approach, where competition is rewarded, it is possible to combine group awards with recognition of individual effort. An analogy would be the teacher who is complimented on the performance of the pupils. In musical competition, the pupil, the teacher, and also the group which was key to the success all receive kudos. And rightfully so.

Someone famous once said, "It's not how you get a job done, the important thing is to get it done." This is not necessarily so. Being late for appointments, not returning phone calls, and letting correspondence pile up may be a way of weeding out unimportant problems but generally is not the approved management method. It can lead to a bottleneck in total production flow. In addition, it creates ill will and hostility.

We consider people in some parts of the world in a stereotypic fashion. Some are punctual and reliable, while others are supposed to be tardy, sloppy workers. Is it the climate? The culture? The work ethic? Or our wrong ideas? In some situations, changing such work habits is an important assignment for today's manager.

Pressure and strict control may help to effect this change, but there are more positive alternatives. A U.S. developer for a new international resort in Mexico had to employ local workers. They were late, and they violated sanitation laws. His job was to alter this pattern of behavior.

He achieved it, at least partially, by mixing a "good" worker with the "poor" ones, thus setting up a role model to be emulated. Offering bonuses, though not a subtle method, also works, particularly when this reward is given to the group as a whole.

Work habits can be related to personality types, and mismatching a worker with a task can be remedied by reassigning the jobs. Sometimes a person is, or feels, overqualified. The resulting poor performance is a form of protest.

DO YOU THINK OF THE CONSEQUENCES?

Decisions imply consequences. This is one of the most traumatic aspects of a manager's job. If you are part of a group, the responsibility is shared by all. But if you are the manager, the blame or reward of the outcome rests on your shoulders.

One signature can have repercussions that last for years. While you are deciding, you feel godlike power. Although you may be working for a large corporation, the moment you choose one direction rather than another, you are an entrepreneur.

In the future, modern companies will consist of small groups of decision makers. The fear and threat of the anonymous giant corporation will slowly disappear. But can decision making be learned? Of course. Be more aware of subconscious influences when you weigh pros and cons. Listen to your intuition; it is a legitimate force in making choices.

Here is a list of decision-making lessons:

1. *Include emotional factors.*   If you like the excitement of risk and speculation, if you lean toward alternatives that cause your adrenalin to flow, act with full knowledge that your emotions are at work.

2. *Play "what if," but analyze all possible consequences.*   For instance, say you build a company based on the founder's name. What if the founder dies? We had to struggle with this for the Duncan Hines Company The problem was solved by involving a philosophy rather than just a name. The decision was made before the death of Mr. Hines and proved to be correct.

3. *Be aware of the changing world.*   Suppose you borrow money for the company's expansion based on good sales and profit margins. The market turns, tastes change, and you can't pay your debt. The company is at stake. Had your decision included the possibility of future changes in tastes, might you have thought differently?

4. *To risk or not to risk.*   Playing it safe is well and good, but a more courageous competitor might corner the market. Your product would then become obsolete, unsalable. Involvement with some risk might be the wiser decision.

5. *Discussion with trustworthy associates is invaluable.*   Talking over

important decisions helps ensure that you don't overlook important details.

6. *Sleep on it.* We discussed this point earlier. Hasty decisions are often wrong decisions.

7. *Immunize yourself against self-reproach.* Prepare yourself for the feelings of making a wrong decision, but don't let that stop you. Then if the roof caves in, you've already lived through the agony in your mind. Give yourself ten lashes with a wet noodle, and move on to Chapter 2.

CHAPTER
TWO

PLANNING
OR THE LACK OF IT:
A HOT MANAGER'S VICTORY
OR DOWNFALL

HOW WELL DO YOU COPE?

Control. Boredom. Time. How well do you cope? Even a top manager has only limited resources. How you deal with these factors and the aggravation they entail is the primary concern here. Take this small test and let's see how these elements affect you.

┌─ Test ─────────────────────────────────

Select the one answer for each question that best expresses your feelings.

Control

1. Imagine your company to be a pyramid. Which illustration is most correct for you?

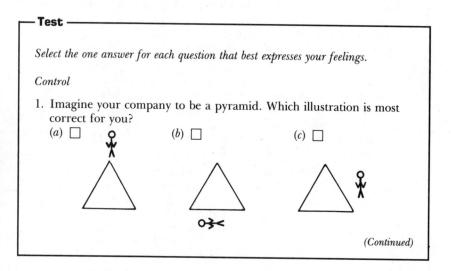

(*Continued*)

---

2. Think of your work during the last month.
   (a) I was always ahead of my assignment.   ☐
   (b) I barely made the deadlines.   ☐
   (c) Work seemed to pile up more and more.   ☐
   (d) Most of the time I finished everything.   ☐

3. Think of your work in relation to you: one cube is you, the other is your work.

| You | Work | You | Work | You | Work |

(a) ☐   (b) ☐   (c) ☐

Boredom

4. Which feeling described here comes closest to your attitudes regarding the length of a workday?
   (a) Every day seems to have 16 hours.   ☐
   (b) I am glad when the day is over.   ☐
   (c) There are never enough hours in the day for me to finish everything.   ☐
   (d) I always find something stimulating.   ☐

5. Here are several ways of making your coworkers more interested in their jobs and performance. Which one would you choose?
   (a) Give them time off to work on extra projects. ☐
   (b) Give them tight schedules.   ☐
   (c) Establish challenging competition.   ☐
   (d) Surprise them with interesting events.   ☐

Time

6. Which principle do you use most in organizing your time?
   (a) I do the most difficult or unpleasant things first. ☐
   (b) I do the things I like best first.   ☐
   (c) I alternate between easy problems and unpleasant ones. ☐
   (d) I do whatever presents itself first.   ☐

7. How much time did you waste last week during normal working hours?
   (a) Not a minute.   ☐
   (b) An hour a day on unnecessary details.   ☐
   (c) Half a day or more by getting involved in a pleasant chat or hobby.   ☐
   (d) I did unnecessary things, but I don't consider that wasted time. ☐

8. Which of these rules do you apply most to time management according to your own self-analysis?
   (*a*) I always make lists of priorities but usually only for the day. ☐
   (*b*) I have a list of priorities. I do those things which bring me closest to fulfillment. ☐
   (*c*) I try to organize my day. I have a watch next to my phone and reminder labels in my office. ☐
   (*d*) I am sloppy with my time, but I hate to be in a strict time regimen. ☐

9. Which label for a time schedule would you permit?
   (*a*) One hour of dreaming. ☐
   (*b*) One hour for just being myself and doing nothing. ☐
   (*c*) One or more hours every day for exercise during office work. ☐
   (*d*) Time set aside to just chat with coworkers. ☐

Scoring and Interpretation

Control

1. (*a*) = 3	2. (*a*) = 4	3. (*a*) = 2
(*b*) = 1	(*b*) = 2	(*b*) = 1
(*c*) = 2	(*c*) = 1	(*c*) = 3
	(*d*) = 3	

Compute your scores according to the values given in the above key.

The best score is 10. The lowest score is 3.

If you score 8 to 10, you are among the people who seldom get out of control.

A score of 5 to 7 makes you a member of the majority—you are keeping up with the demands most of the time.

A score of 3 to 4 is low. You are either not organizing your time well (see time test) or not particularly interested in your work (see boredom test).

Boredom

4. (*a*) = 1	5. (*a*) = 4
(*b*) = 2	(*b*) = 1
(*c*) = 3	(*c*) = 3
(*d*) = 4	(*d*) = 2

Compute your scores according to the values given in the above key.

(Continued)

The best score is 8; the lowest is 2.

A score of 6 to 8, particularly combined with a higher control score, shows good work involvement.

A score of 3 to 5 shows you need more enthusiasm.

A score of 1 to 2 might indicate that your job is not challenging enough.

Time

6. $(a) = 4$ $(b) = 3$ $(c) = 2$ $(d) = 1$
7. $(a) = 2$ $(b) = 3$ $(c) = 1$ $(d) = 4$
8. $(a) = 2$ $(b) = 3$ $(c) = 4$ $(d) = 1$
9. $(a) = 3$ $(b) = 4$ $(c) = 2$ $(d) = 1$

Compute your scores according to the values given in the above key.

The best score is 16; the lowest, 4.

If your score is 13 to 16, you accept the modern view that sometimes supposed wasted time can be productive and that it is not absolutely efficient to get tied down by time schedules. Even dreaming can be helpful.

Keeping Control. Three phones are ringing; letters need answering; and bill collectors are knocking on the door. Are you in a panic? As a top manager, you can't afford to be. You are the hero, the cool person who sorts things out. You fight off wrinkles, pain, and disaster. But when a file is lost, an appointment forgotten, or a phone call missed, it makes you crazy.

Basic training of managers should include comportment in panic situations. Since panic is highly contagious, staying in control is extremely important. The French say, *"Jamais deux sans trois"* (disasters always come in threes). In such panicky moments you may believe this, without realizing you are setting up the third mishap yourself.

Boredom: The Insidious Disease. Without challenges, hours at work loom endlessly, stretching over the horizon in a cloudy haze. Some top managers bristle with excitement while other unmotivated ones act sedated. Often you don't realize that boredom is the virus which has invaded your system.

Boredom is a deadweight that pulls you down until you drown in inertia. Without continuing challenge, not only the job but life itself becomes meaningless. A coworker who has lost the love for work cannot perform properly.

Wasting Time Constructively. Napoleon once said, "I can give you anything you want, except time." One major complaint of most managers is lack of time. Although they have cut unnecessary phone calls and delegated tasks to associates, still there is never enough time to finish all the work.

Time is the raw material at the disposal of managers. They should always be aware of how much time they have, but they should not become obsessed about its limitations.

What would Einstein say about the relativity of time? Your plane has been delayed; the waiting time seems endless. Often what appears to be wasted time on the surface is time well spent.

I was trying to put a chip into my computer. The so-called expert did not know what to do. I called the factory, recorded the detailed instructions, and successfully installed the chip myself. Was it a good use of my time? Possibly not. But I harvested a previously unknown pride and much valuable information about the computer. And this pride gave me energy to tackle other tasks.

How about you? Suppose a brilliant idea flashes through your mind while you are waiting at the airport. How do you qualify this time? Relaxing is valuable in its own way. It lets your mind clear so that new ideas can flow.

Motivation and emotion are important factors in time management. We can live for 20 years doing the same thing, becoming dull from the monotony. But if we do twenty interesting things in a year, it's like living 20 psychological years.

Do we really finish familiar assignments faster? Probably not. Getting involved in challenging and difficult work can shorten time—real and imagined—needed to accomplish a task. So remember, assessment of the ability of prospective employees to manage time should include these factors, perhaps previously overlooked.

Control, Boredom, and Time Management

A top manager must feel like a pilot. Every business is subject to waves in the ocean of events. Keeping the ship afloat without panicking makes a steady guide.

So, we see that control, boredom, and time management are more dependent on freedom and imagination than on regimentation. How do top managers free themselves? Here is some practical advice:

1. Study the biographies of famous people. Churchill was also a painter and a bricklayer. Even during the heaviest blitz, he took a nap

every day. Einstein played the violin. Make room in your day for relaxation, for a change of pace.

2. Invent new challenges. Emphasize the need for new tasks. Practice creative discontent. Avoid reaching dead ends even if others call it success.

3. Eliminate the words *not interested* from your vocabulary. If you don't understand something, learn about it.

4. Tackle one problem at a time. Conquer the unconquerable bit by bit. A former student of mine was ready to give up his quest for a Ph.D. When I visited him, I found all the textbooks lined up on his desk. I removed all but one. He was immensely relieved and assured me he could easily master that one. When that was accomplished, I brought him the next, etc.

5. Translate a large task into a set of small tasks. I once hired a bulldozer operator to dig a parking lot on a steep incline. He refused. So I asked him to open a place at the edge of the hill. Now his machine was horizontal, not tilted, and he continued with the project. His fears were based on the unusual slant. Once the job had been broken down into smaller sections, he was reassured and completed the job.

ARE YOU DRIVING IN REVERSE?

The future is frightening—a dark abyss, a door which opens only outward. Imagine the year 2010. Will the world be better? What will business be like? What new products will exist? What industries will have perished? We'd all love to look in a crystal ball. For a manager, a bit of "futurology" is almost a necessity. But what happened to the good old days? Feeling that things were better then may simply be an unwillingness to anticipate the unknown.

How do you feel about it? Let's find out.

Test

Select the one answer for each question that best expresses your feelings.

1. You read a report by the Club of Rome predicting that the world will become overpopulated, polluted, and crime-ridden and that everything will become automated. Humanity as we know it today will have been replaced by cruelty. What is your most likely reaction?

   (*a*) Grossly exaggerated. ☐

   (*b*) Quite possible. ☐

(*c*) They are right. □
(*d*) They like sensationalism—things will be better. □

2. What do you think the world will look like 20 years from now?
   (*a*) I hope I'll be alive; wonderful things will happen (diseases will have diminished, there will be more leisure time, genetic engineering, no hunger, no wars, travel by missiles, etc.). □
   (*b*) The world will have been destroyed by a nuclear war. If not, there will be overpopulation, nature will be ravaged, and giant megalopolises will cover large stretches of the world. □
   (*c*) Things will be pretty much the same, but we will have learned to use scientific advances to control many problems. Literacy will be universal. Nationalism will be only symbolic, so there will be no nuclear war. □

3. The world of today is like
   (*a*) □   (*b*) □   (*c*) □   (*d*) □

4. The world of tomorrow will be like
   (*a*) □   (*b*) □   (*c*) □   (*d*) □

5. Which of the following predictions do you think will come true in the future?
   (*a*) We will swallow pills of compressed vegetables, meat pills, and tea or coffee tablets. □
   (*b*) More individualism will prevail. There will be fewer products for the mass market and more products for those interested in psychologically and socially different market segments. □
   (*c*) Regular space trips for fun and exploration will be available for the average person. □
   (*d*) Cities like Mexico City and others will be so polluted and have so much traffic that they will collapse and will have to be abandoned. □

6. Changes in lifestyles, morality, and politics will occur. Which do you foresee as most likely?
   (*a*) People will work only 4 days a week—perhaps 3—and enjoy more leisure time. □
   (*b*) Marriage will be a personal arrangement, without any necessary legal or religious sanctions. □
   (*c*) There will be less hierarchy in large corporations. □

(Continued)

(d) Employees will be selected by their psychological inclinations rather than their abilities. ☐

7. What will the market and the economy of the world be like 10 years from now?
   (a) New markets, brought about by new ideologies and more leisure time. ☐
   (b) More inflation, high interest rates. ☐
   (c) More unemployment, caused by robots and automation. ☐
   (d) More restrictions, government control, and/or trade barriers. ☐

8. How will people change as coworkers and managers?
   (a) Companies will be split into self-sufficient small units. Only general services such as accounting, legal services, and advertising will be centralized. ☐
   (b) Unions will become all powerful and actually want to participate in management. ☐
   (c) Less work will be done; productivity will further decrease. ☐
   (d) The United States will become a leader again in innovation and productivity but will share this position with other countries. ☐

9. Politically and militarily, what will happen?
   (a) One of the two superpowers will dominate the world, by blackmail, complacency of the opponent, or military victory. ☐
   (b) Both philosophies of communism and capitalism will converge. There will be no conflict, only revisions and compromise on both sides. ☐
   (c) World peace will prevail and we all will be free to move around without worrying about political powers or military might. ☐

Scoring and Interpretation

1. $(a) = 4$	2. $(a) = 3$	3. $(a) = 2$	4. $(a) = 2$	5. $(a) = 2$
$(b) = 3$	$(b) = 1$	$(b) = 3$	$(b) = 3$	$(b) = 3$
$(c) = 1$	$(c) = 2$	$(c) = 4$	$(c) = 4$	$(c) = 4$
$(d) = 2$		$(d) = 1$	$(d) = 1$	$(d) = 1$

6. $(a) = 4$	7. $(a) = 4$	8. $(a) = 4$	9. $(a) = 1$
$(b) = 2$	$(b) = 2$	$(b) = 2$	$(b) = 2$
$(c) = 1$	$(c) = 1$	$(c) = 1$	$(c) = 3$
$(d) = 3$	$(d) = 3$	$(d) = 3$	

Compute your scores according to the values given in the above key.

The highest score is 34; the lowest is 9.

A score of 27 to 34 indicates a positive attitude toward the future. You don't believe that the world is coming apart at the seams. Such an attitude is very important for a manager, who has to plan ahead.

A score of 21 to 26 puts you still among the futurists although you have some doubts, depending on the areas where you picked a less definite view about the next 10 to 20 years.

A score of 14 to 20 shows that you have doubts about where the world is going.

A score of 9 to 13 shows you are a definite pessimist.

You might want to read *Optimism One* by F. M. Esfandiary.[1] The author reminds us that people used to work 7 days a week, child labor was common, and big cities such as London, Paris, and Berlin were much more polluted 100 years ago. Horses with carriages were the major means of transportation, and the excrement attracted flies. There was no Environmental Protection Agency.

So, are you an optimist or a pessimist? Some optimists believe science will have solved many problems. Optimism obliges action. Pessimism should not be used as an excuse to sit still. Good management requires hope, belief in the future, and dynamism.

Much depends on your age. But optimists can look forward to a promising world even after 80 years of age—and even though they might not be around by 1990 or later. Keeping a diary with clippings about genetic engineering, NASA flights, and new laser technology will help you to convince yourself that people are gradually moving toward progress.

As a planner, such positive expectations can be of great help to you.

ARE YOU COUNTING ON YOUR ANALYSIS OR JUST MUDDLING THROUGH?

Some of the latest research in the field of management raises the question, Is it desirable to approach managerial problems in a planned, systematic fashion or to rely on serendipity, coincidence, and creative disorganization? It is difficult to decide which method works better. There are positive points in both schools of thought. What is important,

---

[1] W. W. Norton, New York, 1970.

however, in managing yourself and others, is making use of your inclination and potential.

This test is designed to find out with which work method you feel most comfortable.

Test

Select the one answer for each question that best expresses your feelings.

1. A new vaccine against an unknown virus is needed. Scientists all over the world try to work out the problem. Finally the answer is found. Who and what method worked, according to your guess?
   (a) A systematic, step-by-step sifting through all possible analyses of the nature of the virus and laboratory experiments was performed until the effective vaccine was discovered. ☐
   (b) Folklore methods and even opinions of primitive medicine men were looked into. It was indeed a medicine man who suggested the right approach which was later scientifically proved right. ☐
   (c) A group of international biologists and health specialists had tried in vain. Then, by sheer serendipity, one spilled a few drops of a completely unrelated liquid into the virus culture and discovered that the virus was destroyed. ☐

2. Up to 80 percent of the latest developments which have led to financial success were brought about by women and men who
   (a) Were almost fanatics and believed in their own final success. ☐
   (b) Combined stubbornness and real know-how. ☐
   (c) Fooled around in their garages or workshops, tenaciously pursuing possible solutions without any real plan. ☐
   (d) Were well-trained scientists who were also creative. ☐

3. You see a sign on someone's desk saying "An orderly desk is a sign of neurosis." Which would you do?
   (a) Laugh and take it as a joke. ☐
   (b) Think that there is some truth to it. ☐
   (c) Absolutely reject it. ☐
   (d) Wonder whether it is merely an excuse for sloppiness. ☐

4. A coworker or associate is being described to you as follows. Which description gives you the most comfortable feeling?
   (a) Rolls with the punches, is disorganized, but somehow gets things done. ☐
   (b) Makes lists and seems to have everything well-planned. ☐
   (c) Is slightly crazy—no one can predict his or her behavior. ☐
   (d) Relies on instinct, leaves everything to the last minute; nothing is properly tested. ☐

5. You are offering someone in your organization a new job. The titles and job descriptions are as follows. Which would make your associate happiest?
   (*a*) Vice president in charge of dreams. ☐
   (*b*) Systems manager. ☐
   (*c*) Vice president in charge of customer relations. ☐
   (*d*) Vice president in charge of research and development. ☐

Scoring and Interpretation

1.	2.	3.	4.	5.
(*a*) = 3	(*a*) = 1	(*a*) = 2	(*a*) = 2	(*a*) = 1
(*b*) = 1	(*b*) = 2	(*b*) = 1	(*b*) = 3	(*b*) = 4
(*c*) = 2	(*c*) = 4	(*c*) = 3	(*c*) = 1	(*c*) = 2
	(*d*) = 3	(*d*) = 4	(*d*) = 4	(*d*) = 3

Compute your scores according to the values given in the above key.

The highest possible score is 19. The lowest is 5. We gave the highest score to answers that indicate an attitude favoring a logical approach.

Therefore, a score of 16 to 19 makes you a member of the logical group.

A better score is lower than this—from 10 to 15. It could be composed of proper mixture between reliance on systematic approaches and belief in intuition and serendipity.

A score of 5 to 9 puts you into the other extreme—those who favor muddling through as being equally effective as using step-by-step procedures.

The method which is most appropriate depends on the problems and, most importantly, on the real inclination of the person in charge. It may help to split the assignment between two or more people who have different approaches.

Many of the great discoveries, such as of the structure of DNA, the famous double helix by Nobel Prize winner James D. Watson, are the result of a mixture of guesswork and experimentation. The atomic bomb was developed by assuming that experiments which should have been the basis of further steps had already been completed—which is utterly contrary to the cause-and-effect type of physics learned in school. Instead of certitude, assumptions of fictitiously finished experiments were used to build the next steps of research.

You should know your preferred working method as well as those of your associates. It is possible to be overorganized and too systematic, particularly when creative decisions are needed.

NEVER MIND YOUR TITLE—ARE YOU ON THE TOP OR THE BOTTOM?

A modern manager should be efficient, experienced, and organized, but at the same time capable of "imperfections." This may sound like a contradiction, but it is a requirement of the future. To avoid prejudicing your answers, take the test first; then we'll explain.

┌─ Test ───────────────────────────────────────

Select the one answer for each question that best expresses your feelings.

1. You discover that your associate keeps a diary on a half-hour basis. What is your reaction?
   - (a) It's a good idea if it's done consistently. ☐
   - (b) Probably he or she is on and off. I start one myself, but then I neglect it. ☐
   - (c) I think it's a waste of time. Things have a way of changing too much anyway. ☐
   - (d) It's ridiculous. There is no privacy left. ☐

2. Do you keep a calendar?
   - (a) I use it only to look at today's date. ☐
   - (b) Yes, also for next year and the year after. ☐
   - (c) My calendar is kept up to date for a month, but not more. ☐
   - (d) I don't even have one! ☐

3. When you are about to visit another company's offices and don't have exact instructions on how to get there, what do you usually do?
   - (a) I ask for exact instructions and mark them on a road map. ☐
   - (b) I just drive more or less in the direction where I remember their offices are—and I often get lost. ☐
   - (c) I stop on the way a few times and ask for directions. ☐
   - (d) I have a good sense of orientation and seldom get lost, even in foreign places. ☐

4. You plan to have things done for a particular day or week.
   - (a) I usually get things done as I planned. ☐
   - (b) It hardly ever works out as I planned. Something always goes wrong. ☐
   - (c) I plan in such a way that there is leeway for some changes. ☐
   - (d) I hardly ever make any plans. ☐

5. You have the following tasks to accomplish. Arrange them in the order by which you get them all done in the least time and without mishaps.
   (*a*) Pick up a parcel. It is heavy, and the place closes at 11 A.M. ☐
   (*b*) Buy ice cream cake to take home. ☐
   (*c*) Stop at the bank to get money. ☐
   (*d*) Stop at a gas station to fill up. ☐
   (*e*) Have glasses repaired. The optometrist promised to have them ready in an hour if they are dropped off in time. ☐
   (*f*) Pick up a customer at the railroad station. The train arrives at noon. ☐
   (*g*) Pick up repaired glasses. ☐

Scoring and Interpretation

1.	2.	3.	4.	5.
(*a*) = 3	(*a*) = 2	(*a*) = 2	(*a*) = 3	(*a*) = 1*
(*b*) = 2	(*b*) = 1	(*b*) = 1	(*b*) = 2	(*e*) = 2
(*c*) = 4	(*c*) = 4	(*c*) = 4	(*c*) = 4	(*c*) = 3
(*d*) = 1	(*d*) = 3	(*d*) = 3	(*d*) = 1	(*a*) = 4
				(*a*) = 5
				(*g*) = 6
				(*b*) = 7

*This version scores 5 points. Pretesting showed, however, other alternatives. If the order permits ice cream to melt or taking too long or missing a closing date, each mistake counts for one point to be deducted from the total score of 5.

Compute your scores according to the values given in the above key.

The highest score is between 17 and 21. In some cases we granted a lower score for a too perfect and almost compulsive solution, although it sounded like a more perfect answer. For example, in item 1(*a*), half-hour diaries are overly efficient; item 2 (*d*) received a 3 despite the apparent inefficiency; and item 3(*c*) was granted a score of 4 because it permitted some inefficiency.

A score below 17 shows too little planning.

We were also guided by our pretesting. Some degree of inefficiency seems to be desirable according to the newest ideas in modern management. We recommend, therefore, that top managers permit themselves a degree of freedom without compulsion. They can compare results of such leeways in themselves and others to rigidity, which only looks like efficiency.

In *The World after Oil*,[2] Bruce Nussbaum states that we are entering an entirely new period in international relations. He predicts that those countries which have not been able to switch from heavy industry based on cheap oil and energy to electronics and information-dominated economic organization will fall behind.

He unexpectedly includes modern Germany among the countries which will suffer this fate. One of the underlying reasons for Germany's inability to move forward may be that the German tendency toward perfection and order that worked so well in a mechanical era is actually a liability in this period of electronics. In microelectronics, imperfection actually has to be built in. Redundancy is inserted into microchips so that when some circuits burn out or fail, others are already in place to pick up the streaming electric current. Any attempt to build the perfect chip produces delays that can put behind the next generation coming off the assembly line.

Thus, efficiency and perfection may not be interchangeable. Planning must leave gaps for expansion—as in a concrete floor. The manager should leave possibilities for sudden changes due to unexpected events.

Coworkers must be trained to take over for others even though completion of these tasks is not in their job definitions. In imperfection we find the seeds of perfection, and thus we can find the motivation to work and think harder to achieve higher goals and find new solutions.

DEVELOPING PATIENCE

Management takes time. Often results are not immediately observable. Patience is related in meaning to the ability to suffer, thus, the words *patient* and *patience*. How do you react to delay? Let's find out.

Test

Select the one answer for each question that best expresses your feelings.

1. You are waiting for an important call. It does not come. How are you most likely to react?
   (*a*) I set a time limit. ☐
   (*b*) I keep on calling. ☐
   (*c*) I give up. ☐
   (*d*) I send a letter or cable. ☐

---

[2] Simon & Schuster, New York, 1983.

2. Your staff member keeps on sending reports that are unsatisfactory. What is your honest reaction?
   (*a*) I blow my top and send back the report. ☐
   (*b*) I sit down with the coworker and try to help. ☐
   (*c*) I give the assignment to someone else. ☐
   (*d*) I decide to finish it myself. ☐

3. Which factor is most important in planning your company's future production schedule?
   (*a*) Likely delays due to human failure. ☐
   (*b*) What the competition will do. ☐
   (*c*) Disasters, weather, and strikes. ☐
   (*d*) Personal failures and delays. ☐

4. Which habit do you have? (Choose one.)
   (*a*) I turn to the end of a whodunit and skip the text in between. ☐
   (*b*) I turn to another channel on TV if the current one does not interest me. ☐
   (*c*) I prefer to pass another car even though it is dangerous. ☐
   (*d*) I wait in line for tickets, no matter how long it takes. ☐

Scoring and Interpretation

1. (*a*) = 3   2. (*a*) = 1   3. (*a*) = 3   4. (*a*) = 1
   (*b*) = 2   (*b*) = 4   (*b*) = 1   (*b*) = 2
   (*c*) = 4   (*c*) = 3   (*c*) = 2   (*c*) = 3
   (*d*) = 1   (*d*) = 2   (*d*) = 4   (*d*) = 4

Compute your scores according to the values given in the above key.

A score of 12 to 16 indicates you tend to wait things out, you accept delays as normal.

A score of 8 to 11 describes you as fidgety, trying to reduce waiting time.

A score of 4 to 7 shows you as decidedly impatient, often with yourself.

As we get older, we learn that it often pays to wait things out. Impatient managers are more likely to make wrong decisions. Deliberately adding several days or hours to urgent problems often results in pleasant surprises.

Patience is a characteristic of adulthood. Freud distinguished between the pleasure and reality principles. Wanting something *now* is a sign of childlike behavior. Being able to postpone the pleasure and reap the benefits later reflects the reality principle. Many management experts claim that this is also the difference between the Japanese and the Americans. We go for the monthly profit statement, while the Japanese realistically invest and plan for long-range goals.

In staffing your department and the boardroom, you need to attract people who can wait, who can plan with long-range goals in mind. Sometimes present staff will need retraining, which requires patience. And then, quite suddenly, someone will reach her or his potential before your eyes and your time will have paid off. Future employees should be evaluated for their capacity to look ahead and discover the means of turning their dreams into reality.

Here are some practical lessons on how to add patience to your busy life:

1. Find tasks to bridge the frustration gap while you wait for a project to mature.
2. Pencil in a delay time on all lists and calendars.
3. Keep a diary which reminds you that goals *will* be reached sooner or later and that later isn't necessarily bad.
4. Distinguish between actions that can be used to speed up achievement of goals and those which are outside your influence.
5. Associate with patient people. They are often calmer and more self-assured.

We all have built-in time clocks. Westerners have one that usually runs fast. Different cultures have other paces of life.

Ms. Greene, a manager, was transferred from Chicago to Lagos, Nigeria. An important meeting was scheduled for 9:30 A.M., but Mr. Nbobo did not arrive until 11 A.M. From that point, everything became an entanglement of delays, overlaps, and confusion. Instead of managing, Ms. Greene was managed, and when she returned to Chicago, she found she had developed a new sense of patience.

You, too, can cultivate this important aspect of managing. Here are some practical lessons:

1. Build in an extra half-hour for delays. Schedule activities to fill in this time. Instead of this time being wasted, it will be productive.
2. Slow *your* time clock at certain intervals. Tell yourself to slow down. Reduce frustration, decrease stress.
3. Take action in another area. Just as pacing is used to siphon off impatience, set aside tasks to fill in such unavoidable delays.
4. Install a slow-ticking clock!
5. Use self-hypnosis techniques to calm yourself.

6. Think back. Does a minor delay *really* make a difference in the overview of a project? Can you remember when it did?

ARE YOU AN INTUITIVE PLANNER?

In effective planning, all possible factors are taken into consideration. But, no matter how careful you are, you may still make a wrong decision. Some managers depend on their intuition to arrive at goals. They roll with the punches. In the end, they feel they are just as well off as the rational manager. How do you fare? Take this test and let's see.

┌─ Test ─

Select the one answer for each question that best expresses your feelings.

1. The salesman visits your offices, trying to sell you a new copying machine. He tells you that he has a special offer if you sign today. Although you really don't believe him, you are still tempted and go ahead. What are your thoughts afterward?
   (*a*) I should have thought it over.   ☐
   (*b*) It probably was the right decision anyway.   ☐
   (*c*) It was the best deal I could have gotten, even if I had shopped
         around.   ☐
   (*d*) I felt bad for a few days; I wish I could have canceled the
         deal.   ☐

2. You are considering the purchase of several computers. The general prediction is that prices will come down. What decision do you make, and what arguments do you use?
   (*a*) Even if prices do come down, I will have lost the use of the
         computer in the meantime. The labor savings will have made
         up for the money savings.   ☐
   (*b*) I believe in always taking the bull by the horns. It was one less
         decision to make.   ☐
   (*c*) I cannot always wait for the best opportunity.   ☐
   (*d*) I felt that my intuition served me right.   ☐

3. You were responsible for the introduction of a new product. You got the go-ahead from your boss, but sales of the product did not get off the ground. Describe your feelings.
   (*a*) I wish top management had restrained me more.   ☐
   (*b*) I am grateful that I had the freedom to make mistakes.   ☐
   (*c*) I was guided by my gut feelings.   ☐

(Continued)

(d) It was still the right plan and product. Perhaps it was premature, or not enough time was allotted for the marketing strategy. ☐

4. Out of nowhere, a new brand of merchandise is introduced to the market by the competition. It seems to be increasingly successful, and you can't understand why your loyal customers are switching brands. What is your strategy most likely to be?
   (a) Start a public relations campaign appealing to the loyalty of my customers. ☐
   (b) Try to find some negative points about the new product. ☐
   (c) Blame my associates for not having been alert enough to anticipate the success of the competition. ☐
   (d) Conduct a thorough examination into the possible explanation of this threat to my market position. Then I choose the strategies to counteract it. ☐

5. Best Food launched a new evaporated milk after exhaustive market tests. Best Food milk tasted much better than the others on the market. It was being used for the preparation of baby formulas. Almost all mothers of young babies declared their preference for this new brand; yet when it was finally brought to the market, it flopped. What could have been the reason? Check the answer which best explains this marketing failure.
   (a) The evaporated milk lost its taste after a while. ☐
   (b) It was too expensive. ☐
   (c) The babies did not like it. ☐
   (d) The mothers had no confidence in the product. ☐

Scoring and Interpretation

1.	2.	3.	4.	5.
(a) = 2	(a) = 2	(a) = 1	(a) = 4	(a) = 2
(b) = 4	(b) = 3	(b) = 4	(b) = 3	(b) = 1
(c) = 3	(c) = 1	(c) = 2	(c) = 2	(c) = 3
(d) = 1	(d) = 4	(d) = 3	(d) = 1	(d) = 4

Compute your scores according to the values given in the above key.

The highest score possible is 14 to 20. This indicates that you are guided by intuition more often than by facts and are capable of unusual solutions.

A score of 9 to 13 shows that you prefer a middle-of-the-road approach.

A score of 5 to 8 classifies you among rational managers who do not rely too often on intuition

It may be necessary to change plans midstream. An "aha" experience—seeing the possible solution in a flash—makes it easier to do that. If plans have been too rigid, we may hesitate in bringing about necessary change. We are more interested in sticking to the carefully plotted scenario. A plan can be a scaffold or a prison for our actions.

Many business (and real) battles have been lost because the leaders did not want to admit that they might have been wrong. By sticking with the plan, they hoped the mistakes would miraculously disappear.

Sometimes, as in the planning of new-car models, it is very difficult to change even the smallest detail. Detroit has finally been sold on compact cars. Suddenly, people in the United States prefer large cars again. Often trends are wrongly interpreted because the planners did not take into consideration the subconscious psychological factors that swayed their decisions.

Planning automatically involves some form of predicting the future. Say the demand for video games increases. You assume that demand will continue indefinitely, but you do not take the fatigue factor into consideration.

You have been struggling with a problem. It seems impossible to find the answer. Stepping aside and rearranging the way you look at the puzzle permits the correct solution to surface. This is called *upside-down thinking*, or serendipity.

There are examples in most unexpected areas. An architect had difficulties with the terrain while building a large structure, so he decided to construct it from the top down, literally letting it "hang from the rafters." A farmer was tired of bending to milk the cows, so she constructed a ramp, let the cows do the walking, and did her chores from a more comfortable position.

Companies get into trouble because their managers are often incapable of approaching problems in an innovative and unusual fashion. Using intuition can also be the wrong approach. What is right? Know what forms of planning are preferred. Gather all the facts, give your intuition free rein, and then take action. Being able to free yourself from the cobwebs of erroneous thinking permits you to cut the Gordian knot.

PLANNING AND HOW TO IMPROVE IT

By now, you should know quite a bit about yourself as a manager. For instance, do you delegate authority properly, or do you try to do everything yourself? Are you efficient, patient, and adaptable? Are you an intuitive or a rational planner? How do you feel about the future?

You may excel in some of these areas, but no one can be perfect in all.

Delegating Authority

Delegating authority is a universally accepted practice. If you have difficulty doing so, it may be due to fear. You feel threatened. You rationalize by saying, "I am surrounded by idiots." But subconsciously you are afraid that the person to whom you have delegated the task is more efficient than you and might through her or his success, endanger your job. How should you handle such fears?

1. *Set your sights on a better position in the organization.*   When your delegate performs well, she or he will actually be pushing *you* up the corporate ladder.

2. *Broaden the scope of the job delegated.*   Create a difference between your job and that of your delegate. Create a mutual learning situation rather than a threat.

3. *Analyze the techniques used by the delegate.*   Was the problem approached from a new angle? Learn from the situation. Discuss it. Perhaps you can work together on the next project and both jump ahead as a team.

4. *Give your subordinate a new title.*   The job is now different—not a copy of yours.

Fear of the Future

Planning of any kind involves, at least partially, the use of a crystal ball, tea leaves, Tarot cards, and/or many other similar devices. A manager consults financial experts, from fundamentalists to technical advisers, and a long list of specialists for any major corporate venture. You want to create tomorrow's headlines but are afraid at the same time. After all, look at the Roman Empire, Napoleon, and the Edsel!

What should you do?

1. Look at the future as a spiral, a seashell so to speak, thesis followed by antithesis, resolved by synthesis. The future is an ever-changing mobile, dangling by a thread but capable of infinite variety.

2. Think positively. This may be easier than it sounds. Remember, predicting doomsday eliminates action. It is often an excuse for laziness. And what is the purpose of worrying? What does it accomplish? Nothing. Once you believe this rationale, you can learn to overcome your fear of the future.

3. Make high technology your friend. The same technology which caused many difficulties in the automated world can be turned around and used for greater productivity. You might find that computers and other automated equipment threaten your coworkers' productivity. It is

important to reassure them that technology can free them to do more creative thinking. Not only is time saved, but entirely new functions can be performed. And wear and tear on people and machines are reduced.

4. Pay more attention to individual work styles, even moods. Modern establishments will create a greater quality of life and enrichment of work through understanding patterns of work-related behavior.

5. Collect clippings on recent discoveries (genetic engineering, elimination of diseases, laser technologies, angioplasty, synthetic insulin, etc.) to make yourself aware of the positive aspects of the future. Look at 1990 or 2000 positively. See "future bliss," not future shock.

THREE
CREATIVITY
THE HOT MANAGER'S KEY TO INNOVATION AND PRODUCTIVITY

WHAT IS YOUR CREATIVE STYLE?

We are all creative, but not all in the same way. Modern management cannot survive without the daily ability to create something new—even if it is merely the result of recombining elements into different forms. Why assume that only artists are creative? Why are they different from the scientists or researchers or managers? The following tests serve only as an indication of your particular creativity. However, we have given you scores based on comparisons with about 200 other managers whom we pretested.

Test

1. You are the buyer for a department store. You have sent out questionnaires advertising the new fall collection of blouses and skirts. Of the 1000 people who responded, 400 want blouses, 300 want skirts, and 150 want both blouses and skirts. The remainder want other types of clothing. What would *you* order?

(Continued)

2. You want to streamline and cut costs in your department. Which managerial solution would you choose?
   (a) Fire people. ☐
   (b) Have customers do part of the work. ☐
   (c) Eliminate services. ☐
   (d) Cut out frills. ☐

3. How could you give staff members a greater feeling of respect for their individuality and privacy? Choose one.
   (a) Invite employees to decorate equipment and machines with graffiti. ☐
   (b) Give personal names to equipment. ☐
   (c) Permit the painting of equipment in preferred colors. ☐
   (d) Offer the possibility of picking furniture from various models in storeroom for employees' offices. ☐

4. An Italian manufacturer of men's custom-tailored suits discovered (through research) that more men were buying ready-made suits. What would be the most creative marketing concept?
   (a) Join the trend and switch to ready-made suits. ☐
   (b) Benefit by the fact that many men are still interested in expensive custom-tailored suits, although the trend is going in the opposite direction. Cater to the lucrative, although diminishing, market. ☐
   (c) Combine both trends. Offer tailored suits with a variation. Basic measurements are taken from a catalog with predetermined sizes. But the customer can then add his own wishes as if the suit had been custom-tailored. The customer comes in for one or two fittings. ☐

5. You discover that almost 50 percent of the owners of private homes with garages seldom put their cars in the garage and leave them outside instead. How can you use this discovery to sell a new product? In each case you would provide the corresponding new products. Choose one.
   (a) Design a cover for the car, and develop a new room out of the unused garage. ☐
   (b) Substitute a carport for the garage, and thus create an extra room. ☐
   (c) Put an indoor swimming pool in the garage. ☐
   (d) Set up a garden, using artificial lights in the unused garage, thus creating a greenhouse. ☐

6. Burlington Industries needed new ideas for their textile designers. What did they to do to stimulate their creativity?
   (a) Set up sensitivity training seminars which could serve as sources for design ideas and develop all the five senses. ☐
   (b) Send the designers to a museum to study other cultures and designs. ☐

(c) Teach them dreaming and "imaging." ☐

(d) Have them study designs in nature, animals, flowers, and landscapes. ☐

7. Your company is stuck with a surplus of sun umbrellas. What can you do with them? Think of entirely different applications utilizing their basic function. Choose one.

(a) As a cover for plants in the garden during hot season. ☐

(b) As small sails for canoes. ☐

(c) As decorations for ceilings in stores or homes. ☐

(d) As advertisements by putting a message on them and displaying them or giving them away. ☐

8. You are a manufacturer of roofing material. What is the best way of stimulating sales?

(a) Add new qualities such as insulation factors to the roofing paper. ☐

(b) Call it something else, such as *home protection*. ☐

(c) Offer it in different colors, to indicate the individuality of homeowners. ☐

(d) Sell initials or special designs to put on the roofing material to beautify the often neglected roof. ☐

9. You are a tire dealer. You have been taking back a large number of old tires. You can't give them away. Using your imagination, what could you do with them? Choose one.

(a) Sell them as flower beds after having them painted in bright colors or providing customers with the paint. ☐

(b) Make swings out of them, and sell them after some minor adaptations. ☐

(c) Suggest that they be used as fences or bumpers in the garage. ☐

(d) Make cushions out of them for indoors or outdoors. ☐

10. Study these designs and incorporate each into an illustration of your own. You might change the square to a cube, draw something inside them, or add to the outside.

(a) ☐   (b) ☐   (c) ☐   (d) ☐

11. If you had to switch around your staff or coworkers, who could do different jobs? Imagine you managed a hotel, for example. Draw lines from the workers to the sorts of work they could change to (match column *A* with column *B*).

A	*B*
(*a*) Salesperson	(*a*) Sales
(*b*) Repairer	(*b*) Repairs
(*c*) Supervisor	(*c*) Supervising
(*d*) Welder	(*d*) Welding
(*e*) Reception desk clerk	(*e*) Reception work

12. Being able to communicate nonverbally involves the use of symbols and the understanding of subtle aspects of abstract and creative thinking. Try this test. Match the drawings in (*a*) to (*c*) with the "words" in (*A*) to (*C*). Use as a comparison the sound, symbolism, or signs.
    (*A*) Roro ___   (*B*) Mo-om ___   (*C*) However ___

13. It helps sometimes to understand the "soul" of the product. Most people do subconsciously associate a gender with a product, even an industrial one. What do you think most people would associate with these products as far as sex (gender) and appeal are concerned?

	Sex	*Appeal*
Boat	Female	Protection
Coffee		
Valve of irrigation system	_____	_____
Irish whiskey	_____	_____

14. Which symbol for progress would you be most likely to choose?

15. Write in the appropriate color:

Danger_____
Distance_____
Peace_____
Caution_____
Wealth _____
Purity_____

16. Match each word in column *A* with one word in column *B* by joining with lines:

A	*B*
Umbrella	House
Woodpecker	Dragon
Inflammation	Digestion
Fireplace	Typewriter

17. You have been offered a new job. You are, however, not very familiar with the operation line of the company. How would you be most likely to go about familiarizing yourself with their specialty?
    (*a*) I first gather general background information. ☐
    (*b*) I prefer to inquire about specific problem areas and try to find answers to the more detailed questions. ☐
    (*c*) I study the history of the company, its origins, and developments. I think about its present and future. ☐

We have used the various tests to determine your specific style. Some people are particularly good at solving practical problems.

Items 1, 2, 9, and 17 are designed to measure this quality. If your answers go beyond the banal and indicate unusual yet simple solutions which can be easily overlooked by others, your strength lies in the pragmatic field, in areas of modern engineering, production, systems analysis, and communications.

The second category concerns the use of intellectual creativity. Items 4, 5, 11, and 12 are designed to measure this form of creativity. They require the ability to shift, to apply logic without being hampered by rigidity. Professor Gordon Pask, a British computer scientist, describes two subdivisions of this intelligence—the groupers and the stringers. The *groupers* are the deductive thinkers who begin with the whole; the *stringers* are the inductive thinkers who proceed step by step and eventually pull in thoughts that relate to the whole.

Artistic creativity is the third category. Here the stringers are prominent. Really intelligent managers free themselves from the straitjacket of purely deductive thinking to see how the parts relate to the whole. Items 3, 6, 7, and 10 are designed to measure this ability.

Wordless-thought creativity is measured by items 8, 13, 14, 15, and 16. Einstein described this ability in the following way: "When I examine myself and the method of thought, I come to the conclusion that the gift of fantasy has meant to me more than my talent for absorbing positive knowledge." [1] His discovery that a light beam could be bent and appear

---

[1] B. Ghiselin, *The Creative Process,* New American Library, New York, 1952.

curved was based on wordless thought when he imagined himself in an elevator moving with high velocity and envisioned in it a beam of light that curved as the elevator moved. Einstein's conclusion was that gravity was capable of bending a beam of light. Anticipating the competition's reaction in your mind by using an image of clever generals in a battle would be a managerial form of wordless creativity.

Scoring and Interpretation

1. The correct answer is 550 blouses, 450 skirts, and 150 other types of clothes. If this is your answer, give yourself a score of 5; if anything else, 0.

2. $(a) = 1$
   $(b) = 4$ (such as filling out order blanks themselves or reading electric meters, if your department handles the use of electricity or water, for instance)
   $(c) = 3$
   $(d) = 2$

3.	4.	5.	6.	7.
$(a) = 4$	$(a) = 3$	$(a) = 1$	$(a) = 4$	$(a) = 4$
$(b) = 3$	$(b) = 4$	$(b) = 2$	$(b) = 3$	$(b) = 1$
$(c) = 2$	$(c) = 2$	$(c) = 4$	$(c) = 2$	$(c) = 3$
$(d) = 1$		$(d) = 3$	$(d) = 1$	$(d) = 2$

8.	9.
$(a) = 2$	$(a) = 4$
$(b) = 1$	$(b) = 2$
$(c) = 3$	$(c) = 3$
$(d) = 4$	$(d) = 1$

10. (a) If you completed the circle ... $= 1$

  If you made a pipe ... $= 2$

  Anything better or more creative ... $= 3$

  (b) ... $= 1$

  Anything better or more creative ... $= 3$

  (c) If you made a cube ... $= 1$

  If you made a picture frame ... $= 2$

  Anything better or more creative ... $= 3$

  (d) If you filled in the triangle ... $= 1$

  If you made a mountain or pyramid ... $= 2$

  Anything better or more creative ... $= 3$

11. The best possible answer, shown here, scores 5. Deduct 1 point for each different answer.

        A   *B*

(*a*) Salesperson   (*a*) Sales

(*b*) Repairer   (*b*) Repairs

(*c*) Supervisor   (*c*) Supervising

(*d*) Welder   (*d*) Welding

(*e*) Reception desk clerk   (*e*) Reception work

12. The best possible interpretation is (A)–(a), (B)–(b), (C)–(c); it scores 3 points each, for a total of 9.

    (B)–(a) = 2

    (B)–(c) = 1

    (C)–(a) or (b) = 1

    (A)–(b) = 2

    (A)–(c) = 1

13. Score 3 points each if you filled in the following: Coffee, male, relaxing; valve, female, delicate; Irish whiskey, male, unaltered. Deduct 1 point for each for anything less creative.

14. (*a*) = 2

    (*b*) = 3

    (*c*) = 1

15. Danger: red; distance: black; peace: blue; caution: yellow; wealth: green; purity: white. This answer scores 3 points. Deduct one point for anything less creative.

16. Umbrella–house; woodpecker–typewriter; inflammation–dragon; fireplace–digestion. This solution scores 3. Anything less creative requires deduction of one point.

17. (*a*) = 2

    (*b*) = 3

    (*c*) = 1

Compute your scores according to the values given in the above key.

The total best score is 84. This means that you are creative in all four areas of technical, intellectual, artistic, and wordless imagery.

To find in which areas your creativity lies, you should add the scores of special tests.

For pragmatic intelligence, add scores of items 1, 2, 9, and 17.

For intellectual creativity, add scores of items 4, 5, 11, and 12.

For artistic creativity, add scores of items 3, 6, 7, and 10.

For wordless imagery, add the scores of items 8, 13, 14, 15, and 16.

The highest score for pragmatic intelligence is 16; for intellectual creativity, 22; for artistic creativity, 24; and for wordless imagery, 22.

To conceive of things as *wordless imagery* is to fantasize or imagine a situation in your mind, without concrete facts—to follow a hunch. The inventor, developer, and scientist use this ability. Hypotheses are drawn from many different sources. An inventor then deduces, debates, turns things around, and finally puts an idea to the test.

Even Michelangelo tested the concept of the *Pietá*. First he made sketches; then he showed them to people and assessed their reactions. He acted as a scientist first and creative genius second.

In a modern company, many styles of creativity are needed. There are at least four major styles of creativity (and *remember*, creativity is *independent* of intelligence):

1. Technical and pragmatic creativity
2. Intellectual creativity
3. Artistic creativity
4. Wordless imagery

Some people have combinations of innovative abilities. Others have only one. Often creative abilities overlap. Hitler hired Albert Speer as his munitions minister even though Speer was an architect. Hitler's explanation was that Speer could think three-dimensionally. He could develop a manufacturing concept step-by-step, the way a building was constructed, floor-upon-floor.[2]

Generally speaking, technical creativity is needed in solving engineering problems such as developing new machine tools or sturdier, more economical packaging. Intellectual creativity is useful in computer programming and more effective cost accounting, while artistic creativity is used in a myriad of dynamic ways. In advertising, designers, art directors, and layout artists must be top-notch to succeed.

HOW TO DEVELOP YOUR CREATIVITY

There are at least four types of managerial creativity: pragmatic creativity, intellectual creativity, artistic creativity and imagery.

Pragmatic Creativity

There is more demand today for engineers with ideas than for those with purely technological knowledge, and this preference applies in almost every field.

General Electric has a whole division devoted to the application of new

---

[2] Albert Speer, *Erinnerungen [Memoirs]*, Verlag Ullstein GM. B. H., Frankfurt, 1969.

plastic, which is as strong as steel. Car engines made almost entirely of plastic represent one possibility.

Could new materials be used in your field? How? What about wider, longer, deeper bathtubs? How about using siphons to pour liquids instead of conventional tilting and spilling? Can water pipes be wrapped in thermostatically controlled heated cables to prevent freezing in winter? Can cars have expandable luggage racks on the roof? How about suburban mailboxes with lights that flash when mail is delivered?

Whatever your field, many million-dollar businesses have been created by applying creativity and thinking unconventionally in otherwise dry, technical areas. Look around you: the improvements apply from thumbtacks to toilet paper (this was an assignment for us by a large paper company). Liquid soap is an old and yet new technically creative idea. So is administering drugs through skin patches to avoid stomach irritation.

Intellectual Creativity

"New math" is a good example of intellectual creativity that uses symbols as abbreviated forms of writing. We already use & to replace the word *and*. Why not carry this further? Do books have to be so cumbersome? Could they be scrolls? Calculators should be built into desks. Problems to be solved could pop out of a desk drawer automatically, one at a time. Documents could be projected onto a wall and studied more comfortably.

The whole area of communication can, and will, be rethought. The writing and answering of letters have not progressed very far since the Middle Ages.

Managers, especially those in multinational companies, should know foreign languages. How can this be facilitated? Hire foreign secretaries who will speak in only their native tongues for an hour or two a day. Use videotapes and cassettes as well as guest lecturers to broaden horizons. A large food company arranged trips to Europe, Japan, and Indonesia to help its managers develop their knowledge of and taste for foreign foods.

Artistic Creativity

Every fashion house needs new ideas. For Burlington Industries, we arranged seminars and nature trips. Fashion designers learned from the shapes, sounds, and feel of the world around them. New ideas blossomed. We asked them to develop "Mozart and Beethoven designs"—translating melodies into form.

Artistic creativity applies not only to packaging but also to technical design. General Electric wanted to convince engineers that a 5-horsepower motor does not have to be enormous. Designing a small model that gives a feeling of concentrated power was the artistic challenge.

Wordless Imagery

Drawing from the fantasy world, we see that imagery is basically a series of "suppose" ideas and experiments. A mother complained that her child was a chronic daydreamer. This is a common complaint, but this time it was a most uncommon child. His name: Albert Einstein. Unfortunately, too often we are stopped from developing such "child-like imagery." What would the world be like if Einstein hadn't persisted in retreating to his fantasy world?

An ideal creativity training course would consist of exactly such imaging. Suppose all the roofs in your neighborhood were different colors? Farfetched? Sure. But we sold this idea to a roofing company!

How about showers in rainbow colors? Keep your staff interested and alert with ideas such as these. You only need one multibillion-dollar idea to ensure your place in history!

UPSIDE-DOWN THINKING—A STIMULUS TO CREATIVITY

International Environmental Dynamics, Inc., is said to be saving $1,000,000 and 5 to 7 months' time by constructing a building from the top down, with each of the twenty floors put together on the ground and then jacked into place. This unusual complex in the Riverdale section of New York City will provide homes and schools for USSR families who are employees of the United Nations.

What is really interesting about the project, however, is that the basic idea is apparently a very practical one, but it hasn't occurred to very many people—at least in this country—to use it extensively.

Daily life is full of possibilities like this one. To take advantage of them requires looking at things upside down, or backward, as in a mirror. This aspect of innovative thinking has also been termed the *penicillin approach* in honor of Alexander Fleming's inspired decision to look at the fungus instead of worrying about the bacteria that it killed. Sometimes we are hindered in approaching a problem in the new way because it defies tradition.

The Forest Lawn Cemetery in the Los Angeles area is one place where a new idea has definitely been put into effect. Here, the customary rows of prestige-advertising monuments and statues have been replaced by simple blocks sunk into the ground. In addition, benches are provided, and there is soft background music. So the entire expanse of this large, beautifully landscaped cemetery has been opened up and made conducive to quiet reflection and enjoyment of nature.

This is a much more natural, and certainly a much more dignified, way of contemplating death than is possible in the traditional cemetery. It is not surprising that at least part of the Forest Lawn Cemetery plan is being adopted elsewhere. However, with some bold thinking, this same idea can be carried still further.

There is no reason, for example, why people have to be buried lying down. Instead they could be sunk into a shaft, thus taking up less space in crowded urban cemeteries. This is almost literally upside-down thinking! To be sure, such a method of burial would be in direct contradiction to our fondness for thinking of death as eternal sleep—one does not ordinarily sleep standing up. So if we tried to persuade people that vertical burial might be desirable, we would inevitably run headlong into emotions that would constitute a real obstacle.

To be creative successfully, we must learn to overcome this sort of resistance, which is often subconscious, whether we encounter it in ourselves or in those whom we want to convince. Look at farming. The typical farmer has a more or less inborn notion that a field must be plowed in nice, straight furrows. Yet for farmers who have been persuaded to try new ideas, contour farming has proven value. The fields may look untidy, but farming in this way is a lot more practical and comfortable.

On a much smaller scale, suppose you want to save soap—a worthy goal at any time. Now, soap holders have been built into bathroom tiles and kitchen sinks for years, and countless others are available in local department stores. But if you aren't careful, the holders fill up with water and eventually become encrusted with wasted, expensive soap. A solution used in some public places, particularly in Europe, is to attach the soap to a string, so that you wash your hands by rubbing them against a kind of soap "pendulum." There is no danger here of the soap melting away, as it does in most soap dishes, although possibly four out of five people would insist they couldn't use "soap on a string."

Suppose you want your next office party to be a winner. Turn your thinking upside down. Give people badges or other means of identification—humorously done—that not only supply names but also cue people as to professions or even hobbies. Conversation and contacts will be easier.

Make it a habit to apply upside-down thinking, or mirror imaging, to such business problems as product development and improvement, sales promotion, systems analysis, and employee training. Learn the basic art of asking questions. You may occasionally make listeners speechless at your apparent insanity. But don't worry about this. The trouble lies in the tendency of people to assume that so many subjects are not open to question or discussion. But can't they be?

Here is a test designed to measure your ability to exercise new forms of creativity as a top manager.

Test

1. How can you improve the cutting of cumbersome, large plywood sheets which take up large amounts of space?

2. You manufacture hay balers. The farmer has to turn around each time to see how well the machine works. How can this be avoided?

3. You are managing the office of Canadian tourism. Which concept of Canada held by U.S. travelers do you have to change and how?

4. Best Food launched a new evaporated milk after exhaustive market tests. It tasted much better than the ones on the market. It was being used for the preparation of baby formulas. Almost all mothers of young babies declared their preference for this new brand. Yet when this milk was finally brought on the market, it flopped. Check the answer which, in your opinion, best explains this marketing failure.
   (a) The evaporated milk lost its taste after a while. ☐
   (b) It was too expensive. ☐
   (c) The babies did not like it. ☐
   (d) The mothers had no confidence in the product. ☐

5. A greeting card company knew that the major market for a resale approach of their cards was comprised of middle-aged women who split the profit with their churches or charitable organizations. The company used testimonials showing typical women of this group, who told of their successes. The problem lay in how to expand the

market. What had been wrong in the company's reasoning? How should the company have best expanded the market?

(*a*) By increasing the profits made by the women selling cards. ☐
(*b*) By improving the designs of the greeting cards. ☐
(*c*) By finding out the real reason why these women sold the cards. ☐
(*d*) By looking for the people who might have similar motivations
for making money. ☐

You have two ways of testing your ability to do upside-down thinking: (1) You can do it unaided, by putting down your own ideas. (2) You can use our checklist, marking the answer(s) which seem(s) best to you.

We will then give you the scoring of your answer.

Scoring and Interpretation

1. Close to our solution = 3
   Otherwise = 0
2. Mirror = 3
   Otherwise = 0
3. Map of Canada like our suggestion = 3
   Otherwise = 0

4. (*a*) = 2   5. (*a*) = 1
   (*b*) = 3   (*b*) = 2
   (*c*) = 1   (*c*) = 3
   (*d*) = 4   (*d*) = 4

Compute your scores according to the values given in the above key.

In item 1, our solution was to stand the sheet of plywood up and use a saw to cut vertically down the sheet. If your answer is close to our solution, your score is 3, for your ability to do upside-down thinking.

In item 2, our solution was to install a mirror next to the operator of the hay baler so there will be no need to turn around. If your answer is close to our solution, you score 3.

In item 3, our solution was to draw the outline of a map of Canada which fills the whole chalkboard and puts the United States at the bottom. This prevents what happens when the borders of Canada are put at the upper edge of the chalkboard. Most Americans, that is, those living in the United States, drew a map that left enough room for the United States on the chalkboard. Thus the tourist office manager will need to do real upside-down thinking to get Americans to think of Canada as a completely separate country with its own worthwhile differ-

(Continued)

ences. This would have to come first, before praising the beauties of Canada.

If your own answer was close to our solution, give yourself a score of 3 for your ability to do upside-down thinking.

What was your explanation for item 4? The real reason why the mothers did not buy the milk was that it had not been endorsed by their pediatricians. There was an interesting sidelight. Mothers who had had their first babies were much more negative than those who had their second or third babies.

The highest total score is 17; the lowest, 2.

Thus if you scored a total of 2 to 5, you are not flexible enough to think of unusual solutions to managerial and marketing problems. The next score of 6 to 10 is an average result—nothing special.

A score of 11 to 17, however, puts you in a group of executives who have the ability to think along more innovative and creative channels. By developing this ability and applying it to your company's problems and situations, you can put your talent to creative use.

You can train yourself to think upside down. First, playfully reverse a problem in your mind. Instead of your bending down to milk cows, how about letting the cows walk up a platform so you can milk them while you are standing?

A Mrs. Strout discovered trash farming by simply letting old crops and weeds rot. Not only did they add fertility to the soil, but also she was saved time and energy by not having to clean the garden.

Putting fluorescent lamps into a socket made for incandescent lamps changed the use of these lights, making them acceptable for living rooms, etc. Locating light switches on the floor and door sills avoids having to search for them in the dark. The light is activated automatically when someone enters the room.

Many successful new services and products have been developed in this fashion. Upside-down thinking has many applications. It can save energy and time and improve productivity. The important thing is to resist the human tendency to regard certain concepts as sacred—beyond question—and to begin challenging them from the most extraordinary angles you can contrive.

LATERAL THINKING—A USEFUL APPROACH

Most of us have been taught that the best way to solve a problem is to concentrate until we come up with the right answer. Modern theories suggest precisely the opposite approach.

Lateral thinking is what we are urged to apply; thinking away from our problem—above, below, or around it—just so we stop focusing on it. We tend to hypnotize ourselves. This prevents our seeing the numerous aspects contributing to a final solution.

Unlock your mind. Try this test. Then we'll talk more about it.

Test

Select the one answer for each question that best expresses your feelings.

1. You are interested in developing a new dog food. All possible claims have already been made—more meat, more vitamins, better liked by dogs. Try lateral thinking. Which is the best approach?
   (*a*) Dog food is similar to baby food. ☐
   (*b*) Dogs like bright colors. ☐
   (*c*) Dogs have a keen sense of smell. ☐
   (*d*) Dogs and bones go together. ☐

2. Ask your coworkers which one of these lateral associations they would use for a savings institution.
   (*a*) Savings/rainy day. ☐
   (*b*) Savings/duty. ☐
   (*c*) Savings/freedom. ☐
   (*d*) Savings/fun. ☐

3. Ask your coworkers to draw a line from each subject to the most appropriate association. Write the reason for the association in the third column.

Subject	Creative association	Reason
(*a*) Fire alarm	(*a*) Mother	
(*b*) Grammar	(*b*) Battle	
(*c*) Skiing	(*c*) First love	
(*d*) Penicillin injection	(*d*) Marriage	

4. Ask your associates how to increase acceptance of elderly employees among the rest of the staff. Choose one association that comes to mind.
   (*a*) Sympathy ☐
   (*b*) Insurance ☐
   (*c*) Immortality ☐
   (*d*) Experience ☐

5. Ask an associate to continue the chain of associations with words in the left-hand column, choosing from the accompanying list as a starter. Go as far afield as possible, yet stay within practical applications.

(Continued)

(a) Calendar   Organization of time
(b) Lawn mower   Haircutting
(c) Hat   Fashion
(d) Seeds   Flowers

Use two associations for each subject.

Scoring and Interpretation

1. (a) = 4   2. (a) = 1   3. (a)–(a), (b)–(d),   4. (a) = 1
   (b) = 1   (b) = 2   (c)–(c), (d)–(b)*   (b) = 2
   (c) = 3   (c) = 3   (c) = 3
   (d) = 2   (d) = 4   (d) = 4

*This arrangement scores 4 points. Deduct 1 point for other associations.

5. (a) Calendar: resolution = 3
                 aging = 4
   (b) Lawn mower: neighbors = 3
                   noise = 4
   (c) Hat: decoration = 3
            rank = 4
   (d) Seeds: vegetables = 3
              concentrated power = 4

Compute your scores according to the values given in the above key.

The best score is between 13 and 32, a medium score is 9 to 12, and the lowest score is 6 to 8.

Here is the explanation of our scoring:

In item 1, in an assignment for General Foods we thought about comparing dog food to baby food. There are human mothers and animal mothers. They all are convinced that their babies are unique, particularly bright, certainly cute, and possessing many individual characteristics. As a result, we developed Cycle, which has different recipe combinations for different ages of dogs. Our original idea went much further—we offered dog food for different psychological types of dog.

In item 2, we gave (d) the highest score. We used this approach to stress the idea that having money saved permits you to experience enjoyment and freedom, which received a rating of 3; duty and rainy days were more commonplace associations.

In item 3, fire alarm went with mother, because it protects you as a mother does. Penicillin was comparable to battle, because it fights bacteria.

Skiing and first love may seem dissimilar, but both involve charting new territory—over new snow and just-awakened feelings. Both grammar and marriage connote laws and restrictions.

The idea behind all these applications was to help you see that introducing such apparently illogical connections led to further creative concepts.

The same was true for item 4; it made people think about their own aging and desire to keep active. Helping elderly employees to be hired was stimulated by such motivations.

In item 5(a), a calendar not only suggested resolutions, but also demonstrated how each day added to or took away from one's life. We used this idea to write a motto for an art calendar of a philosophical nature.

In item 5(d), the idea of concentrated power for seeds led us to new forms of advertising for a seed company.

Lateral thinking requires the courage to escape from your immediate concerns and look for other than customary solutions.

Wolfgang Koehler, a German psychologist, defined this ability in the following experiment. A chimpanzee in a cage was given a banana. No matter how far he stretched his arm, he couldn't reach the banana. Now, a stick was placed beside him in the cage. How many apes would starve because they were unable to take their eyes off the banana and think about using the tool to reach the object of their desire?

Once we have been pried loose from the fixation of the systematic and logical approach, the solution seems so obvious and simple that we wonder why we took so long to arrive at it. Try this: What do hotels and anthills have in common? Link concepts that appear at first glance to have no connection at all. The answer is that both hotels and anthills are inhabited by many (or groups of) individuals.

The lateral thinker doesn't concentrate on the logical, systematic approach. First ideas are generated by indirect thinking—thinking through the full range of human needs. When a likely solution has appeared, it is then subjected, by means of vertical thinking, to all logic possible.

Lateral versus Vertical Thinking

Edward de Bono distinguished between lateral and vertical thinking. He described vertical thinking (the traditional method) as placing one stone squarely upon another. It is characterized by continuity, whereas lateral thinking is characterized by *discontinuity*. De Bono spelled out further differences between the two:[3]

1. Vertical thinking chooses; lateral thinking changes.
2. Vertical thinking uses information for its meaning; lateral thinking uses information to trigger new ideas.
3. In vertical thinking, one thing follows directly from another; in lateral thinking, you can leap.

Edward de Bono quite rightly pointed out that most people find it necessary to use both types of thinking. For a rigorous examination of a possible decision or course of action, vertical thinking—firmly grounded in traditional principles of logic—is essential. Yet lateral thinking helps us to escape from the treadmill of old ideas and to generate new ones.

LEARNING TO ASK FUNDAMENTAL (EVEN STUPID) QUESTIONS—THE PATH TO BRIGHT, CREATIVE ANSWERS

A hotel chain is about to construct several new hotels worldwide. Their first approach is to study existing facilities to determine new ways for hotel rooms and services to be organized. This instinctive approach seems logical and natural—it has proved successful in the past.

But one top executive dared to ask, "Will the guests of the future be the same as those today?"

Before we reveal the outcome, take this test which was developed to help you see the value in asking fundamental questions. Learn how you, too, can learn to use this dynamic tool which is always at your disposal.

┌─ Test ───────────────────────────────

1. What is the real function of a door? How could it be replaced? Put down your ideas and then compare them with our suggestions.

    (*a*) Hot air serves as a curtain; some department stores use it. ☐
    (*b*) Strong lights prevent people from looking in. ☐
    (*c*) White noise is created and shuts out interference by intruders. ☐

2. How could traffic congestion be relieved? What is the real purpose of traffic and transporation? Put down your own ideas and then look at our answers.

---

[3] Edward de Bono, *Lateral Thinking*, Harper & Row, New York, 1971.

(a) Why does everybody have to start and finish work at the same time? Staggering work hours would alleviate traffic congestion and many other problems caused by the present working situation. ☐

(b) The city of Vienna has free buses which go to all the most frequented museums and public places. ☐

(c) Rent cars designed for one person at various places in the city while your big car is being parked for you. ☐

3. Ask your new employees what kind of business they think the company is really in.

Scoring and Interpretation

For items 1 and 2, if you came up with two or three similar or equally good possibilities, give yourself a score of 3 for each. If you developed one possibility, your score is 2. If you could not think of any new idea, your score is 0.

For item 3, the further removed the comparison, the higher the score, because it shows a better ability to think creatively. For example, a special manufacturer is really in the computer field because he or she transposes ideas from mental form to a visible form and permits manipulation.

The score would be 3.

Compute your scores according to the values given in the above key.

The highest score, then, for all three tests is 9. This test is somewhat different in its scoring methods than others.

You must use your own judgment as to your ability to ask fundamental questions.

The better you can apply this method to your own business and operation, the more likely you are to come up with creative new ideas.

Now that you've had time to think about the problem of building the hotel of the future, let's see how your conclusions compare. Running through a list of possibilities, the executive came up with one rather fundamental observation: more female executives will be traveling in the future. Studying the needs of this new market revealed two things. First, it was easier for a male executive to arrange a meeting in his private room than for a female. One solution is to have sleeping and meeting areas separated—an idea quite common in Japanese offices where the working area can be screened off through a parchment soji.

Second, although most phones in the hotel room are near the night table, no space was left to write messages, etc. So the new plans offer the possibility of plugging in the phone in one or two different sites in the room, including the bathroom.

"What are toys?" asked a toy manufacturer whose stock had slipped drastically. The answer included video games and home computers. These "toys" rejuvenated the failing business, and it expanded into new areas of development because of that simple question.

Being able to ask fundamental questions is an important prerequisite for today's executive. A question often helps show a dimension previously overlooked. It helps us find dynamic diversification that can boost sales and energize personnel.

By learning to ask questions (though they may sound stupid at first) you can take on even the most complex problems in a creative fashion. You might instill this habit of going back to basics by asking your coworkers what they consider their jobs to be.

Another exercise is to answer children's questions: Why is the sky blue? Why do people wear the kind of clothing they do? Why do I change from a cranky person to a happy one in the same day?

Cutting through the extraneous data often reveals the answer to the question. Unfortunately, we take too many things for granted. We assume the superficial description is sufficient. *Dig deeper.* Analyze statements and criticially explore things. Don't just accept. People make mistakes.

The first response to your approach may be laughter at the simplicity of your idea. But don't forget that Michelangelo was ridiculed. Look at Leonardo da Vinci and Christopher Columbus—the list is endless.

COMBATING STICK-IN-THE-MUDS

How often have you said, "Whenever I attempt to put a creative new idea across, my enthusiasm is dampened by the pragmatists. They are always ready and willing to cite similar ideas that were tried and failed"?

No matter how creative your ideas are, unless you know how to sell them or how to win over the people in your organization who are ready with pejorative comments, you won't get far.

How good are you at combating stick-in-the-muds? Try this test, and then let's see how you can improve yourself.

Test

Select the one answer for each question that best expresses your feelings.

1. You suggest that fresh rolls be delivered in suburban neighborhoods to private homes from a nearby bakery or food chain. Which objection is most valid, and how would you overcome it?
   (*a*) It will be too costly. ☐
   (*b*) People have breakfast at different times. ☐
   (*c*) Some rolls will be stolen. ☐
   (*d*) We could experiment in one neighborhood first. ☐

2. A bank manager proposes to install a travel department. Which of the following arguments do you find most convincing?
   (*a*) Banking has to be modernized. This is one way to go about it. ☐
   (*b*) There are enough travel agencies. They will scream about unfair competition. ☐
   (*c*) Banks don't have enough space as it is. ☐
   (*d*) Let us call it travel loans and work together with travel agencies. ☐

3. You are a builder. You suggest that changes be introduced into new-home design in order to be competitive, such as extra large bathtubs for two, whirlpools, greenhouses, and extra bathrooms. Use no more bookshelves. Instead, store books on cassettes or on software disks. These are the pros and cons as seen by the architectural firm. With which one do you agree most?
   (*a*) It will increase the cost of the home too much. ☐
   (*b*) People don't want to give up old habits. ☐
   (*c*) Space saving will make up for extra costs. ☐
   (*d*) We don't build today the way we used to 100 years ago. Why not anticipate some future developments? ☐

4. You are in charge of developing scents. The company needs new markets. You are the manager. Your ideas range from odors for clothing to scents to be added to food synthetically, by impregnating paper towels, toilet paper, etc. Here are some reactions. Check the one most like your own.
   (*a*) People are very conservative about odors. They will reject such ideas. ☐
   (*b*) We have to try even "crazy" ideas. We can always adapt them to reality later. ☐
   (*c*) We desperately need new markets, but we should not waste our time and money. ☐
   (*d*) Even the Egyptians used scents for the bath, for the temples. ☐

Scoring and Interpretation

1. (a) = 1	2. (a) = 3	3. (a) = 1	4. (a) = 1
(b) = 2	(b) = 2	(b) = 2	(b) = 2
(c) = 3	(c) = 1	(c) = 3	(c) = 3
(d) = 4	(d) = 4	(d) = 4	(d) = 4

Compute your scores according to the values given in the above key.

The best score is 12 to 16. You are capable of defending your new ideas.
A score of 8 to 11 shows that you don't give up too easily but that you have doubts sometimes.
A score of 4 to 7 indicates that it is not enough to have new creative ideas. You have to learn to sell them.

Our tests indicate there are various ways of defending a new idea. We can suggest the following:

1. At least experiment and give the idea a chance. Should it work, you can develop it further and use it in various broader fields.
2. Carrying an idea to its extremes is another way of combating stick-in-the-muds. It is a way of saying "OK." Accept your objection, but then assume that the worst happens. Anticipating the worst outcome can often help in getting a new idea accepted. Citing examples from the past, even from history, can offer a convincing argument.
3. Pointing to future developments by introducing dynamic thinking can be a persuasive argument.

Everywhere, we steadfastly defend customs without ever dealing with the impracticalities. We work unquestioningly from 9 A.M. to 5 P.M.; we insist on Saturday and Sunday as our days off; we docilely endure bumper-to-bumper traffic and late train schedules; we trudge silently through miles of airport corridors with back-breaking suitcases.

Anyone directly concerned with promoting change of any kind knows how tough myths are to break. Whether it is a new product, a new attitude, or an entirely new lifestyle—it will be opposed. What's more, the opposition will include a number of so-called experts who will cite overwhelming statistics. They will conclude with certainty that your proposal is downright crazy or, at best, impractical.

It might be interesting to keep a list of "facts" and "statistics" offered in support of cherished beliefs. How many stand up under close scrutiny? Which are real and which are myths?

The top manager can use a number of techniques to develop innovative thinking in a general and practical way:

1. Upside-down thinking
2. Lateral thinking
3. Combating stick-in-the-muds

Okay, let's assume you've got a great new idea. It's a winner and you know it, but it contradicts everything your organization stands for. What should you do? What follows can be used as a possible guideline for putting a proposal across.

CREATIVITY FOR THE HOT MANAGER

Now that you have ascertained your style of creativity and tested some techniques, here are some additional twists which you can use to live up to your reputation as a hot manager or to teach others.

Experimenting

You are convinced that your idea has value. Don't give up without a struggle. Remember, not only may your opponents be armed with nonfacts, but also your own mental arguments *against* the idea may be erroneous. Something that appears to be fact may not really be a fact at all.

So many new ideas are dreamed up, yet few (no matter how zealous their originators may be) turn out to be worth anything. "I receive ten new ideas every week" is what a research and development expert or new-products manager will tell you. Multiply this figure by the number of companies, and you begin to understand the situation. There seems no end to new ideas—from a lightweight plastic car to a funeral registration bureau in Washington where people could place their last wishes on record.[4]

The important point with any approach is to rehearse it in your mind. What will the idea actually entail? What will you do if it's accepted? Where will you start? Mentally rehearse every detail. All too often, this mental planning is overlooked.

For example, you want a different job. So you apply and are accepted

---

[4] This idea was inspired by a story about the late President Franklin D. Roosevelt. Weeks after he was laid to rest in Hyde Park, it was learned through a handwritten note that he wanted to be buried elsewhere!

for a new position. But now you are disappointed. Why? Because you never took the time or trouble to imagine in detail the change in advance. You neglected mentally some aspect of the real, total experience.

Whenever feasible, follow up mental experimentation with physical testing. This will help you get closer to the actualization. It may be a paradox that creativity is a scarce commodity, while you are surrounded by people constantly dreaming up new ideas. But creating is not enough. You must market your idea. To do that, you must be fully aware of all aspects—pros, cons, practicalities, drawbacks. You put your idea on the line and stand behind it—that is creativity.

Testing the Extremes

"Yes, but. . . ." Does this sound familiar? You may have come up with a unique approach to your business. But the people who work with you may very well object to your thinking. They may ridicule you. How do you cope with this reaction?

Before you meet such a challenge head on, realize that deep inside you are bound to have doubts. How do you know your idea will succeed? You don't. So you test it.

Testing the extremes means you carry the idea to the most exaggerated lengths without, of course, wasting a lot of time or committing unreasonable amounts of money. Determine whether, in actual practice, the idea is ridiculous. Then, for good measure, take exactly the opposite point of view and see how that works. You can't expect success every time. Think how gray and uneventful your days would be if everything worked out as you imagined.

Sometimes people advocate the most grandiose ideas and attempt to put them into effect without testing the extremes. Utopians and Orwellians who dreamed over the years of the ideal world have made this mistake. Perfect communities (such as New Harmony, Oneida, Walden or Walden II) have tried sincerely to base their thinking and planning on the best scientific principles. But when they set about translating their perfectly organized world into reality (with all its numerous details), they ran into unaccountable and insurmountable obstacles.

Indeed, how dull a perfect world might be. Just imagine if everything functioned smoothly, without the least effort. Suppose there were no problems to solve, no tasks to complete, no discoveries to make. We would be so bored!

The point is this: Do *not* discourage your creative potential. Do the opposite. Testing your thinking will give you courage to confront your opponents.

Dynamic Thinking

A particularly stubborn form of resistance to new ideas is called *hindsight*—looking backward. People who indulge in this practice collect innumerable data on what worked and didn't work in the past. Hindsight is the *opposite* of looking ahead, of projecting one's thinking into the future, of thinking dynamically.

A great deal is published these days on the dangers that loom ominously over us all in this modern world gone haywire. TV commentators and their guest experts speak gloomily of uncontrollable bouts of famine. What these pessimistic clairvoyants don't realize is that the human mind and spirit have the ability to counteract. The more threatening the situation may be, the more inventive we become.

For instance, we are thinking in dynamic new ways about solar energy as a substitute for conventional fuel sources. Instead of worrying about overpopulation, we have reduced population growth in the United States to practically 0 percent in a few short years.

Dynamic thinking means taking into account the possibility of new discoveries and inventions, new applications of present knowledge, technological developments, new philosophies and attitudes. Heart transplants have been done for only a few years, and now there are artificial hearts. Physicists conjecture about space colonization. What next? Far from running out of food, we need only to harvest the abundant sources of nourishment in our oceans.

Our minds must be trained to look ahead. Remind yourself of the many things that didn't exist a short decade ago. What would Rip Van Winkle say about such everyday phenomena as video games, home computers, television, jet planes, air conditioning, frozen dinners, synthetic fabrics, and plastics?

To get your new ideas translated into reality, you need *staying power*. In dynamic thinking, you often are recycling old concepts once regarded as impractical. You must convince yourself and others that what you're proposing is worth trying. Top managers have to defend their ideas.

CHAPTER
FOUR
EMOTIONS
AND CONTROLLING THEM:
A HOT MANAGER'S
BATTLEGROUND

ARE YOU REALLY HAPPY IN YOUR JOB?

Why are there so many plays with a main topic of getting out of the rat race? Retirement is being described as finally being able to do what you really want. Does this mean that all these years you have hated what you were doing? Being unhappy with your job can affect your managerial success. Your own unhappiness can carry over to your associates. Find out what your true feelings are. Take this test.

Test

1. Close your eyes. Forget the problems of finding a different job, relocating, learning a new skill. You are doing something that makes you feel really excited. Check the answer that fits your feelings best.
   (*a*) It would be something completely different from what I am doing now. ☐
   (*b*) It would be doing the same work I am doing now, but part-time. ☐
   (*c*) It would be learning more about my work, doing the same thing but better. ☐
   (*d*) I am happy with what I am doing. I wouldn't want to change. ☐

2. You are told that a friend has switched from being an art director to a hair stylist, and he explains this change in the following ways. Which reason would you accept most readily?

(Continued)

   (*a*) I did it only because I can make more money. ☐

   (*b*) I am independent. No one tells me what to do. ☐

   (*c*) I am in constant contact with people, rather than being cooped up. ☐

   (*d*) The heads whose hair I treat are like sculptures. ☐

3. You have inherited sufficient money that you don't have to work anymore. What are you most likely to do?

   (*a*) Continue with work as before. ☐

   (*b*) Spend more time with a hobby, but do some of the same work. ☐

   (*c*) Just take it easy and do nothing, except enjoy sports, fun, etc. ☐

   (*d*) Learn something completely different and switch occupations. ☐

4. Try to think of your job in a symbolic way. Which design is closest to your feelings about your present work?

   (*a*) — — — — — — ☐

   (*b*) 〜〜〜〜 ☐

   (*c*) ⟶ ☐

   (*d*) ⟶ ☐

5. What would be your ideal job? Choose one.

   (*a*) It would be very much like my present one. ☐

   (*b*) It would be much more challenging. ☐

   (*c*) It would offer more independence. ☐

   (*d*) My job is what I make of it. ☐

6. Think of some of the happiest moments in your present job, and list them. How many are there?

7. Think of the unhappiest moments in your job. List them. How many are there?

8. You have made a lot of money in one way or another. You don't have to work anymore. What are you most likely to do?

   (*a*) Stop working at my present job and take it easy, enjoy myself. ☐

   (*b*) Develop my hobbies, maybe into a job. ☐

   (*c*) Keep my present job and possibly learn new skills. ☐

   (*d*) Step down a notch below my full capacity and relax more, giving a new employee a chance to learn my job. ☐

Scoring and Interpretation

1. $(a) = 1$	2. $(a) = 1$	3. $(a) = 4$	4. $(a) = 2$	5. $(a) = 3$
$(b) = 2$	$(b) = 2$	$(b) = 3$	$(b) = 3$	$(b) = 4$
$(c) = 3$	$(c) = 3$	$(c) = 2$	$(c) = 4$	$(c) = 2$
$(d) = 4$	$(d) = 4$	$(d) = 1$	$(d) = 1$	$(d) = 1$

6. $1-3 = 2$	7. $1-3 = 3$	8. $(a) = 1$
$4-7 = 3$	$4-7 = 2$	$(b) = 2$
More than $7 = 4$	More than $7 = 1$	$(c) = 4$
		$(d) = 3$

Compute your scores according to the values given in the above key.

You are very happy in your job if your score is between 22 and 31. If your score is only 9 to 13, you would be well advised to either try to make your present work more challenging or switch occupations, once you have figured out what makes you unhappy. It could be having to deal with people or just the opposite.

Items 6 and 7 may be particularly revealing. If the happiest moments consist of appreciation by coworkers and recognition by professional peers, you are people-oriented. If your happiest moments are more impersonal, such as developing a new product, making a better production schedule, or other achievements which involve people only indirectly, then your happiness is more or less independent of people.

Some managers are loners; others need constant contacts.
A score of 14 to 21 can reflect a feeling of flatness [item 4(*a*)], when nothing exciting seems to happen [also item 5(*b*)]. Much depends on the type of job. Sometimes an occupation does not offer enough stress. Stress is a reaction and not necessarily a product of the situation itself.

People sometimes overload themselves with tasks because they are afraid of not being wanted or needed. But the opposite may be true. They may not have enough challenges and may feel frustrated and bored. Job happiness is often a question of attitude.

A depressed manager must learn to reassess the situation. Loss of self-esteem creates negative feelings in a job. Discussion of the limitations of an occupation with colleagues can reveal ways of adding new challenges and ideas. Of course, if nothing works, you may have to consider a new job, to make a crossover, just as the art director became a hair stylist.

Self-fulfillment is a buzzword. "Happy employees make productive workers." This sounds good, but there are at least two problems. Coworkers may not really know whether they are happy. They may say, "Yes, I'm happy." And then, a few weeks later, they leave. Had you known, or had they expressed their dissatisfaction, you might have been able to correct the unhappy situation.

What leads to job dissatisfaction? Among the factors are lack of challenge, overqualification, failure to be appreciated (or imagining so), and being under stress. How does a manager tell when a person is truly happy? Should it make any difference, or should people do their jobs no matter what?

Work enrichment and a high quality of life go hand in hand. Knowing the degree to which a worker is chafing is the first step. Altering that situation so you have a productive employee is the second step. Sometimes it helps just to make the employee aware that it is often an illusion that the grass is greener elsewhere. On the other hand, it's always good to remember that some workers like to be unhappy—maybe even more than you suspect.

HOW WELL DO YOU TAKE CRITICISM?

Is there anyone who likes criticism? Probably not. Receiving criticism is usually an unpleasant experience—one's self-esteem is lowered. The classic reaction is defense. How well people accept criticism depends in large measure on how it is given. And criticism doesn't have to be expressed verbally. Exclusion from an office party and having one's ideas tossed into the trash as unusable are clear-cut forms of criticism.

Yet, criticism is necessary. It is a useful form of communication. If criticism is given fairly and constructively, people are apt to correct their mistakes and make faster progress toward their goals.

The six situations described below will help you find out how well you take criticism. Study the questions below, and check the alternative that most closely describes your reactions.

┌─ Test ───

Select the one answer for each question that best expresses your feelings.

1. You are wearing an unusual red shirt with fancy trim to the office. Your coworkers stop and stare; they point and whisper. How do you react?
   (*a*) Maybe they are right. This outfit is really too zany.   ☐
   (*b*) Those people do not understand good taste when they see it. I like this shirt, and that's what counts.   ☐
   (*c*) Maybe I should have asked someone's opinion about this outfit first.   ☐

2. In the next office, you overhear your boss yelling at one of your colleagues. What is your reaction?

(a) The boss, whether right or wrong, should have spoken quietly. ☐
(b) The colleague should defend his or her position. ☐
(c) It would help him or her to learn to do better next time. ☐

3. You have been asked to write a marketing plan reflecting your supervisor's ideas. You make some minor changes, but upon presentation the boss insists you exactly follow the original proposal. What is your reaction?
(a) I will not change the approach. It's right this way. ☐
(b) I am sorry, I will redo it. ☐
(c) The plan is much better this way. I will try to show its merits. ☐

4. Which statement best describes your own attitude?
(a) By and large, I don't think I have any more faults than the average person. ☐
(b) I have lots of faults and like to have people tell me, so I can improve. ☐
(c) The less I know about myself, the better. Otherwise, I might hate myself. ☐
(d) I don't think much is wrong with me. I really think I am pretty good. ☐

5. At a party, you commit a *faux pas*; you say something stupid. Someone else points it out. What is your most frequent reaction?
(a) I reject the criticism as unfair. There was nothing wrong with what I said. ☐
(b) I would have apologized anyway. There was no need to rub it in. ☐
(c) I was wrong. It just slipped out. I should not have said it. ☐

6. You tell someone about your success and exhibit your work (new product, packaging, organizational chart, etc.). That person says nothing but seems to disapprove. What is your response?
(a) I say nothing, but I feel bad and hurt. ☐
(b) I tell that person what others have said and how they praised my achievement. ☐
(c) I start criticizing and belittling my own work. ☐

Scoring and Interpretation

1.	2.	3.	4.	5.
(a) = 3	(a) = 1	(a) = 1	(a) = 3	(a) = 1
(b) = 1	(b) = 2	(b) = 3	(b) = 4	(b) = 2
(c) = 2	(c) = 3	(c) = 2	(c) = 1	(c) = 3
			(d) = 2	

(Continued)

6. $(a) = 3$
   $(b) = 2$
   $(c) = 1$

Compute your scores according to the values given in the above key.

If you scored from 6 to 9, you can't take criticism and probably won't admit it even if you are wrong.

A score of 10 to 15 shows that you can take criticism if it doesn't hit your sore spots.

A score of 16 to 19 shows you profit from fair criticism that fits your standards, but usually you aren't swayed too easily.

We all have images of ourselves. Yet who wants to look into a psychological mirror? We may not like our voices or our looks, but what we say about ourselves is not necessarily proof of what we really think. Repeating "I am the greatest" can be viewed as a sign of a shaky self-image. Stating our weaknesses may be a form of fishing for compliments.

Having to work with someone who can't take criticism is frustrating. The more violently a person reacts, the more certainly the criticism was justified. Criticism can help us look at ourselves with a more objective vision.

The inability to accept criticism causes us to exhibit resentment; we shift the blame onto others, accusing them of stupidity or jealousy. When we defend ourselves passionately, our weaknesses stand out clearly.

Perhaps this defensive reaction is due to being oversensitive or to a fear of accepting the thankless job of changing and learning. Or the reaction may be due to the manner in which the criticism was given. Constructive criticism pays for itself a thousandfold; it doesn't leave coworkers angry and bitter.

Ideally, everyone should be her or his own critic, setting standards and goals that are reasonable and commensurate with ability. Once a person has learned to judge self-performance, that person is ready to accept *constructive* criticism and reject useless, derogatory remarks. Fair comments should be used to correct and improve. One should not be blown about like a straw in the wind by useless and deprecating remarks.

Factual criticism—which makes you face up to an actual failure—should be heeded. Perhaps you are off track with your goals; perhaps you have been unreasonable with yourself.

"Loose talk" coming freely from others often masks their shortcomings and diverts attention from their own failures.

Last, some people will tease about or criticize something that is out of a person's control (red hair, freckles, etc.). The best way to combat this type of nonsense is to make fun of it yourself. Disarm critics by beating them to the punch!

HOW WELL CAN YOU HANDLE A CRISIS?

A sudden, unexpected event—an accident, the discovery of an incurable disease, or the visit of the president of your multinational company—can trigger a crisis. Sometimes it's an opportunity in disguise.

It is important for managers to be tested: How immune are they to crises? Can they handle a charged situation? These tests are designed to combine your past experience with your perceptions of future reactions.

Test

Select the one answer for each question that best expresses your feelings.

1. One of your clients declares bankruptcy. You and your company stand to lose a lot of money. In all honesty, what are you most likely to do?
   (a) Blame myself for several weeks because I was not more careful. ☐
   (b) Cut my losses and write it off as part of doing business. ☐
   (c) Double my activities to increase business and to make up for the loss. ☐
   (d) Give up my business and turn to something else. ☐

2. You discover that one of your employees has been secretly stealing clients and has established a competitive business. What is your most likely reaction?
   (a) I slander that person to the new clients. ☐
   (b) I offer congratulations. ☐
   (c) I think to myself, fine, who needs disloyal people anyhow? ☐
   (d) I blame myself for not having paid more attention to apparent dissatisfaction. ☐

3. After many years of loyal service, you are fired without warning. It's difficult to find another job in the same field at the same salary. What is your most likely reaction?
   (a) I start a business of my own. I consider the firing a new opportunity. ☐

(Continued)

> (b) I get a job in a different field, while exploring possibilities in my old field. ☐
>
> (c) I blame myself for not having worked harder. I feel depressed because I should have prepared myself for this eventuality. ☐
>
> (d) I try to get back at the company by letting out my anger at them. ☐
>
> 4. You have overextended yourself; your company is underfinanced. In addition, your competitors are determined to see you close down. What will you most likely do?
>   (a) I gain new credit and start over. ☐
>   (b) I go to work for another company. ☐
>   (c) I start a lawsuit against my competitors. ☐
>   (d) I feel beaten. Maybe I'm not an entrepreneur after all. ☐
>
> 5. One of your associates has made a major blunder. Your business (or division) has been seriously hurt. The person is called to task. Which attitude would you find most acceptable in that person?
>   (a) Feeling insulted. ☐
>   (b) Being overly defensive. ☐
>   (c) Accepting criticism, and asking for help. ☐
>   (d) Laughing it off. ☐

Scoring and Interpretation

1. (a) = 2	2. (a) = 2	3. (a) = 4	4. (a) = 4	5. (a) = 1
(b) = 3	(b) = 4	(b) = 3	(b) = 3	(b) = 2
(c) = 4	(c) = 3	(c) = 2	(c) = 2	(c) = 4
(d) = 1	(d) = 1	(d) = 1	(d) = 1	(d) = 3

Compute your scores according to the values given in the above key.

The highest score is 16 to 20. You are capable of selecting the most constructive solution presenting itself in a managerial situation. This is an important ability—a prerequisite for a top manager.

A score of 10 to 15 requires some analysis on your part. Which are the areas that unnerve you? Could you have a tendency to avenge yourself or look for a culprit rather than examining your own behavior?

A low score of 5 to 9 indicates a generally defeatist attitude.

In the business world, a crisis can be triggered by a shortage of materials, the resignation of a top employee who knows details of the operation, deadlines, cash flow problems, and a myriad of other causes.

Some of us hide. We pretend nothing is happening. We look the other way in a childish but symbolic gesture. The difference in reaction to a crisis is the difference between a leader and a follower.

Overreaction is another possibility. In a study for an automobile insurance company, we introduced a stress test to be used when people take the driver's examination. Most accidents occur under stress. And we don't just mean those accidents involving cars. It is important that managers be tested on how they handle unexpected crisis situations.

Preparing an alternate plan of action is an excellent approach. You will not be caught off guard, and you will have that extra edge of confidence so useful in times of crisis. You will be more likely to translate your mental resolve, as indicated by your test answers, into realistic corrective action.

Most managers who were pretested opted for taking decisive action. Of course, that is the correct attitude. However, proposed behavior and actual crisis behavior can be very different!

DOES GAMBLING SCARE YOU?

Why do intelligent people make bad investments? Do they like the excitement, the game, the adrenalin flow? Life is filled with risks. A number of tests have been devised to measure your readiness to take the plunge. Remember, honestly counts!

┌─ Test ─────────────────────────────────────

Select the one answer for each question that best expresses your feelings.

1. You are considering applications for a division manager who will handle advertising and marketing. Which of these prospective employees would you choose?
   (a) Mr. O'Connell, age 41, working 10 years with the company, has an excellent record. He wants to enlarge his area of responsibility. ☐
   (b) Ms. Wong, age 28, with a liberal arts background. She is very creative and somewhat rebellious, and she has no advertising experience. ☐
   (c) Mr. Young, age 32, a fast learner who has had a variety of jobs including sales. However, he has never held a job for more than a year or two. ☐

(Continued)

2. You are approached by an inventor who has developed a new packaging for liquids such as milk so they will not require refrigeration. Your packaging goods company is asked to invest in this new approach and to use it. Limited testing has been done. What do you do?

   (a) I let another food company be the first to experiment. Then, depending on their degree of success, I recommend the idea to my company. ☐

   (b) I help the inventor collect more data and conduct a market test. I introduce the idea to one specialized area for production. ☐

   (c) I take an option on the idea; I am innovative. I don't let the competition get ahead of me. ☐

3. Your facilities are too small. Various real estate brokers and architects are bidding for larger quarters. All things being equal, which offer is most inviting?

   (a) Enlarge the present space by adding several floors, thus retaining the same address and contacts with suppliers and clients. ☐

   (b) Move to another state where land is cheaper. Erect a new expanded building, but risk dislocation of staff, suppliers, etc. ☐

   (c) Buy a white elephant, for instance, a castle requiring extensive remodeling. If this were successful, it would add a unique and positive dimension to the company's image. ☐

4. Your company is involved in medical diagnostic apparatus manufacturing. One day you see an advertisement in the paper: "Physician needs $100,000 to invest in a new diagnostic procedure. Considerable gains assured. Unique approach. Guaranteed to appeal to a large group of medical specialists." What do you do?

   (a) I write for details. Perhaps my company will be interested. ☐

   (b) I distrust such offers. Certainly, a serious inventor would have approached this situation differently. ☐

   (c) I call. Perhaps I will learn something. It could be the product I've been looking for. ☐

   (d) I investigate, but carefully. I've been burned before, but one never can tell. ☐

5. A story appears in *Fortune* magazine describing how Dr. Land started Polaroid with next to nothing, and you have seen similar success stories. What's your most likely reaction?

   (a) It happens one time in a million. ☐

   (b) I'm dreaming too, but I don't have the courage. ☐

   (c) I, too, will succeed, maybe on a minor scale. I have an invention which could make a sizable sum. ☐

   (d) I like to sleep at night. So I might not die rich, but my company will be safer. ☐

Scoring and Interpretation

1. $(a) = 1$ 2. $(a) = 1$ 3. $(a) = 1$ 4. $(a) = 2$ 5. $(a) = 2$
    $(b) = 3$ $(b) = 2$ $(b) = 2$ $(b) = 1$ $(b) = 3$
    $(c) = 2$ $(c) = 3$ $(c) = 3$ $(c) = 4$ $(c) = 4$
                                            $(d) = 3$ $(d) = 1$

Compute your scores according to the values given in the above key.

A score of 14 to 17 shows you or your associates are willing to take risks—a factor considered extremely important in this very competitive business climate. Even bankers apparently are eligible as risk takers.

A score of 10 to 13 indicates answers that require a moderate risk.

A score of 5 to 9 reflects managers who are very cautious.

Our pretest showed that 66 percent chose item 1(*a*), a person offering maximum security. And 66 percent were willing to take a moderate risk by choosing item 2(*b*). In item 3, the sample is divided: 40 percent chose (*a*), a conservative solution; 40 percent were ready to buy a white elephant; only 16 percent were willing to move to another state.

In item 4, 75 percent were willing to meet the inventor physician, choice (*c*). In item 5, 75 percent checked (*c*).

Taking risks involves courage and the readiness to accept criticism when things go wrong. A leader must accept responsibility. In some progressive companies, special training and facilitation in unusual business procedures are part of the basic approach. By allocating a certain amount of money (which can be lost or written off), encouragement for innovation and risk taking is provided. In some areas, such as banking, it has become imperative to come up with new approaches considerably less reliable than those to which bankers are accustomed. Mergers and diversification are more accepted, each requiring business courage and new outlooks.

Distinguish between static and dynamic security. If life is like a rapid stream, then static security is comparable to clinging to an overhanging branch to avoid being swept away. Of course, the branch could break. Dynamic security means letting go—swimming with the current.

Taking risks is one secret of successful entrepreneurs. Taking risks means controlling the fear of failure, which is more damaging than monetary loss. Fear can lead to self-doubt and hesitation. Taking risks may involve sleepless nights, worries, and stress. For some managers it is a necessary condition of the job.

Being aware of the degree of risk you or your associates are willing to take can be crucial. But if you gamble, do it with confidence.

HOW GOOD IS YOUR SENSE OF HUMOR?

Max Eastman, the writer, once observed that almost anything can be humorous. You can watch someone tumble down a flight of steps, and your reaction may be laughter—you are glad it didn't happen to you.

In business, you are often confronted with situations where everything seems to go wrong. Often the best solution is to laugh. How good is your sense of humor? Let's find out.

┌─ Test ─────────────────────────────

Select the one answer for each question that best expresses your feelings.

1. Things have been going badly for your company. You discuss this with a priest who comforts you: In the hereafter there will be no such problems. Everything will be dandy. You meet a rabbi. You tell him of the priest's comforting words. He looks at you and then says, "Will I laugh when there will be just as many problems!" How does this joke make you feel?
   (a) I feel better about my present problems. ☐
   (b) It does not help. I can't laugh about my problems. ☐
   (c) It is a racially prejudiced joke. ☐

2. Two business friends working in the garment industry discuss the sudden death of their competitor. "You mean he dropped dead, just like that?" The other one asks, even more surprised, "What, in the middle of the season?" What is your reaction?
   (a) What am I working so hard for? It could happen to me, too. ☐
   (b) I am going to take my work a little less seriously. ☐
   (c) It is a sad but deeply philosophical joke. ☐

3. There is a definite system of organizing executives who arrive at the heavenly gates. St. Peter asks all those who were dependent during their lifetimes and had to kowtow to clients and bosses to line up on the right. A long line forms. All those who were independent are to form a line on the left. One man stands alone. St. Peter walks up to congratulate him. "What made you stand here?" he asks. "I don't know," he answers. "My boss told me that's what I should do." What is your reaction?
   (a) How true. No one is really independent. ☐
   (b) I probably am kidding myself, too, when I believe that I don't have to listen to anybody. It is not true. ☐
   (c) This doesn't apply to me. I am my own boss. I have no reason to laugh. ☐

4. You receive a card kidding you about your bad habits. What is your most likely reaction?
   (*a*) I resolve to take revenge and play a practical joke. ☐
   (*b*) I show it to my friends and laugh. ☐
   (*c*) I tear it up because I don't want to be reminded of it. ☐

Scoring and Interpretation

1.		2.		3.		4.	
(*a*) = 3		(*a*) = 2		(*a*) = 1		(*a*) = 2	
(*b*) = 2		(*b*) = 3		(*b*) = 2		(*b*) = 3	
(*c*) = 1		(*c*) = 1		(*c*) = 3		(*c*) = 1	

Compute your scores according to the values given in the above key.

A score of 10 to 12 shows your sense of humor is very helpful. Develop it and use it.

A score of 7 to 9 reveals a medium-range ability to laugh and make a joke about yourself.

A score of 4 to 6 says that you take life and yourself too seriously. Norman Cousins claims that he once cured an incurable collagen disease and later the effects of a heart attack by watching old Buster Keaton movies.

Kings had court jesters. It was a great way to rid themselves of stress or tension. A joke at the right time can save you from embarrassment. Humor can lead to a better deal or to reestablishing friendly contact with a coworker.

Jokes usually center on unpleasant aspects of life, such as illness, death, or taxes. This should tell us something about their function.

Laughter lets off steam. It can break the constraining tide of a bad mood or depression. Laughter liberates. Physiologically, it oxygenates the blood.

Perhaps as a modern executive you should have a good joke book on your desk. In fact, when hiring a new employee, you might well include a laugh test—see how lighthearted the person can be. When you are able to see things in a humorous light, your mind works better.

Circulating cartoons around staff offices can change negative behavior. "Five excuses for being late" was a poster which helped eliminate late arrivals. How well do you accept jokes about yourself? Just for fun, write a scenario roasting your life or job.

GRIMACE OR SMILE—WHAT DOES IT MEAN?

My grandson overheard me saying, "I am not in the mood to tackle this job."

"What is a mood?" he asked.

Indeed. What is a mood? It is not a disease; nor can it be measured in the usual way. How moody are you? Does this affect your work? How well do you handle the moods of coworkers?

Test

Select the one answer for each question that best expresses your feelings.

1. Which of the following best describes you?
   (*a*) I have my ups and downs, but I usually come back to a relatively normal level—unless there is a major reason for my depression. ☐
   (*b*) Sometimes I feel that nothing makes sense anymore. I am ready to quit. If you ask me the reason, most of the time I can't really say. Then the mood disappears again without too much obvious explanation. ☐
   (*c*) I always get mad at people who become sullen without any apparent reason. I think they just want to draw attention to themselves. ☐
   (*d*) I am almost always in a good mood, optimistic, and inclined—and often expected—to cheer up others. ☐

2. Which most applies to you?
   (*a*) In the last few months, I apologized to someone for having been in a bad mood and therefore unjust in my judgments. ☐
   (*b*) When everybody seems upset, I join in or to try to correct the situation, pointing out that things are not as bad as they seem. ☐
   (*c*) Counting or estimating my ups and downs in the last 2 months, I consider my depressions mostly a self-indulgence. ☐
   (*d*) I try to figure out where my bad mood might be coming from.

3. Whatever your mood, to what do you attribute it?
   (*a*) Some disturbance in my endocrine system, a cold, or a physical indisposition. ☐
   (*b*) Others' actions. ☐
   (*c*) Myself. ☐

4. What is your reaction to bad news?
   (*a*) I get over it rather quickly. ☐
   (*b*) I go into a depression for a while. ☐
   (*c*) I cheer myself up by thinking about positive events. ☐
   (*d*) I get mad at colleagues. ☐

Scoring and Interpretation

1. (a) = 3   2. (a) = 2   3. (a) = 1   4. (a) = 3
   (b) = 1   (b) = 4   (b) = 2   (b) = 2
   (c) = 2   (c) = 3   (c) = 3   (c) = 4
   (d) = 4   (d) = 2   (d) = 1

Compute your scores according to the values given in the above key.

A high score of 13 to 15 shows that you control your moods or take positive action to prevent negative effects.

A score of 9 to 12 indicates that you have normal ups and downs.

A score of 4 to 8 indicates that you should learn to master your mood swings and avoid using a bad mood as an excuse to shirk responsibility.

A coworker warns, "The boss is in a terrible mood today." A colleague says, "Maybe now's the time to ask for a raise."

A mood is an emotional state, not a mental attitude—although the former can influence the latter. As I explained to my grandson, "Sometimes people are on top of a mountain; at other times they are in a deep valley."

When in a bad mood, we are often inconsiderate, and we criticize other people's work unfairly. Often we are really mad at ourselves, but we take it out on our work, our coworkers, even machinery!

Conversely, being in a good mood may lead us to say yes at an inappropriate time. Take the example of the boss who approves a raise without giving it proper consideration.

Most of the time, we have good reasons for our moods. At other times, they just happen. A good or bad mood can appear from nowhere, for no apparent reason. Asking why the mood exists—investigating all possibilities—is the beginning of a cure.

ARE YOU A SANDPAPER OR BUTTER MANAGER?

Top managers are expected to be optimistic, to plan ahead, to make correct decisions. but, most importantly, top managers must remain cool—in control of the situation—even when others panic. In short, top managers *must* control their mood swings.

Just for a moment, imagine a corporate president sitting at a large conference table. The board of directors is gathered to discuss a multimillion-dollar deal. A decision will be made within the hour.

Unfortunately, the corporate president is in a foul mood, because of an argument she had at breakfast. Is it inappropriate to show this mood? Certainly. Is it damaging? Absolutely. Clearly the president may create an antagonistic mood at the conference table.

Moods are not usually hidden. Workers are very aware of their supervisor's emotional state. Whistling, smiling, a friendly hello, slamming a briefcase down, a sour expression, a curt remark—the signs are there. How guilty are you of forcing your mood on others?

What is meant by the word *mood*? We really don't know. It may have an obvious cause such as failure, bad news, etc. Or, indeed, a mood can be rooted in a deep-seated mental state, such as depression—it is considered the dark side of mania.

High on life and *down in the dumps* are quite accurate descriptions. The Greek philosopher Epictetus once said that people are troubled not by things but by thoughts about the things. In other words, we talk ourselves into or out of our moods. When we are happy, we see the world brightly. When we are depressed, our surroundings appear dark, somber, gloomy.

What Should You Do?

We suggest taking the following approach to mood swings.

1. Have three rubber stamps made that say, "I'm in a good mood," "I'm in a bad mood," and "I'm indifferent today." Before criticizing or analyzing reports, stamp the paper with your mood. This will make your bias clear. This might seem like a joke, but seeing your mood on paper helps you to dissipate your feelings.

2. Look for the cause of your mood. Were your expectations too high? Are your expectations of yourself unreasonable? Did something concrete cause this mood?

3. Take a deep breath and say, "The heck with my negative feelings. I have no reason to be upset." It *is* possible to change your mood at will.

4. List the positive and negative events you have experienced during the week. Is your mood justified? Do you want to stay in that mood, or do you want to reverse the trend?

Separate those negative experiences which can be remedied from those that are beyond your control. This is a powerful and effective tool for mood changing.

Handling Anger

Psychologists have studied the best methods of handling anger. They mention five things to keep track of, perhaps in diary form:

1. Identify the event that may have triggered your anger.
2. Did something or someone cause the reaction?
3. If a person caused your mood, can you avoid contact? Can you prevent a repetition of the event?
4. Register your degree of anger. Try to control it, and record how well you succeed.
5. Review this anger diary periodically with someone you trust. Assess how well you are controlling your anger.

Another effective method is to write a letter to the source of your irritation. Whether or not you send the letter, you'll feel much better for having written it. All too often, we like being angry. It gives us an excuse for pushing others around. Why do we pursue this masochistic/sadistic practice? No one knows. But it has no place in the world of business or top management.

Controlling Worry

Should top managers worry like everybody else? Certainly. But, at the same time, top managers should know the techniques of controlling worry and its effects.

Worrying is comparable to moodiness. It shows an apparent fear of disaster. Handling anxiety is your concern as a top manager. A well-proven method is to list your worries in diary form (or on a calendar). Review it each month. How many of your fears were realized? In most instances, it was a smaller number than you anticipated.

Worry beads are used by Muslims and Greeks; the rosary performs a similar function. If you are religious, pray—but not at board meetings! Praying enables you to share your worries—it makes you feel that you are not alone.

If you are not religious, try discussing your worries with a colleague. We experimented successfully with the establishment of a bar within the office building, to which managers could withdraw (with or without ingesting alcohol) to discuss their problems with peers in a relaxed atmosphere. Being aware that others have similar concerns can be very reassuring.

MOTIVATION

HOW TO MOTIVATE YOURSELF AND OTHERS

ARE YOU AMBITIOUS OR JUST JEALOUS?

Motivation is like a wound-up spring which drives us toward a goal. This impetus is essential to a top manager. In business, hierarchies are established to provide employees with incentives. Managers must be properly motivated themselves in order to motivate others. The following test will help reveal your ambitions.

┌── **Test** ──

1. Mark Chart 1 (page 90) with a red X on the line for the level you have reached so far for each category. Connect them. Then mark with a blue X the levels you would like to reach within 5 years. Connect them as before. The two lines will show the motivational differential. For an explanation, see Scoring and Interpretation. See sample chart below.

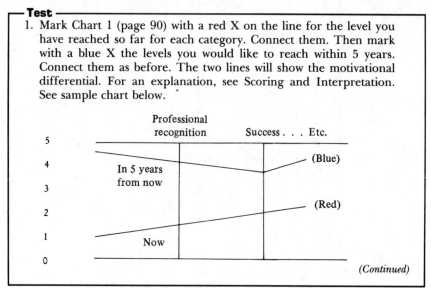

(Continued)

CHART 1

	Professional recognition	Success	Possessions	Money	Adventure	Love	Health	Knowledge	Security	Family life
5										
4										
3										
2										
1										
0										

2. Here are a number of statements made by various people. Which one statement describes you best?
   (a) My goal is to enjoy life as much as possible. I don't want to work too hard. ☐
   (b) I want to earn enough that I can live comfortably and be respected. ☐
   (c) I am always pushing ahead. I go for growth and progress. ☐
   (d) I feel the fun is in the striving, even if you never reach your goal. ☐

3. When you think about the future and your career, what is your usual method for reaching your aspirations?
   (a) I make careful plans, sketching what I have to do step by step. ☐
   (b) I prefer to let things develop by themselves; I believe in good luck. ☐
   (c) I seek out a model, someone whose success formula I can emulate. ☐
   (d) I am satisfied with my present status, so why struggle? ☐

4. Imagine 50 chips are given to you at birth. You can use these chips whichever way you wish. But you cannot have any more during your lifetime. How would you most likely divide them?
   (a) I use all my chips to work toward making more money and being successful. ☐
   (b) I use half of my chips for money goals, the other half for health. ☐
   (c) I divide up my chips evenly among money, professional recognition, possessions, health, love, and adventure. ☐
   (d) I use my chips up as needs arise. When I have used them up, too bad. ☐

Scoring and Interpretation

1. If your goal differs from your present level by 5 points, give yourself 5; accordingly if the motivational differential is 4, give yourself 4, and so on.

   You now do two things: compute the score for each category, such as success, money, etc., and then total the scores.

   If the differential is 5 in all ten categories, your total motivational differential is 50. In other words, you are far removed from having reached goals in all ten categories.

   If your total score is 25, you either are halfway to your goals in all categories or more in some and less in others.

(Continued)

2. $(a) = 1$ 3. $(a) = 4$ 4. $(a) = 4$
   $(b) = 2$ $(b) = 2$ $(b) = 3$
   $(c) = 3$ $(c) = 3$ $(c) = 2$
   $(d) = 4$ $(d) = 1$ $(d) = 1$

Compute your scores according to the values given in the above key.

The highest score is 62.

A score of 40 to 62 puts you in the same group as most top managers. You have great motivational differential and lots of ambiton.

A score between 25 and 39 shows that you have reached your goals in some areas. Thus your motivational differential is reduced (by having achieved your goals), or you are more interested in combining a good life with growth, and letting things develop by themselves, than in pushing too hard.

A score of 12 to 24 shows that either you have a long way to go to reach your goals or you are not particularly ambitious. You seem to prefer a good life rather than success, lots of money, or recognition. Much depends, of course, on your age. Older people will have narrowed the gap between present status and desired goals. The question now arises, Which group is the happier or, more specifically, which will produce a better manager? It is quite possible that people who accept their status and don't try too hard are indeed happier.

Individuals can be ranked according to motivation. Abraham M. Maslow, the well-known psychologist, claims that psychological self-realization is the highest level, while physiological needs are basic motivators. What Maslow and others have overlooked are the dynamic aspects. We are motivated only while trying to reach a goal, be it money, safety, or self-esteem.

Where are you now? And where do you feel you could reasonably expect to be in a number of years? Connecting the points marked for each goal on the scale reveals a continuous curve indicating your aspirations. By marking, on the same scale, where you are now in each category and then connecting these points with a line, you will create a curve reflecting your present situation as you see it. Then compare the difference between these two curves for each goal in turn. You can clearly see the motivational differential. This is what really drives you.

The narrower the gap, the fewer the aspirations. The wider the gap, the greater motivation that is needed.

As a top manager, you push harder, even if not all the goals are reached. You may be under more stress, but stress adds a certain spice to life—it makes daily chores more exciting.

How can you change from a placid, satisfied person to a more aggressive type, or the other way round? Accepting challenge—continuous striving—makes life richer. On your motivational differential scale, as you come close to reaching a goal, set your sights even higher.

Most advertising and religious concepts promise us paradise. If it really existed, it would be a boring place, indeed. The contented person has nothing to look forward to. But top managers are interested in new and different subjects, and these topics do not have to be part of their professional careers.

Johann von Goethe's Faust, while looking for the meaning of life, stated that it consisted of accepting challenges, being discontent in a "creative fashion." Getting there is *all* the fun, not just half of it.

The importance of expanding your horizons, setting higher goals, and establishing new motivational differentials applies not only to you but also to the training and education of coworkers. Help them motivate themselves.

HOW HOT A MANAGER ARE YOU?

A leader must take action, not make pronouncements. The more a manager pulls rank to stress authority, the less a true leader that person is. By the very definition of the word, a manager leads, even at the risk of displeasing some people in the organization.

When a manger moves into this role after having been a follower, her or his outlook must change. We scoured the literature to arrive at a consensus on what leadership involves. There are dozens of definitions from courage to ruthlessness, to choosing the right coworkers. Our tests, based on some of these definitions, should help you determine whether you (or the people you might be considering for this role) have leadership qualities. We'll discuss the results later.

Test

Select the one answer for each question that best expresses your feelings.

1. Something has been misfiled or done incorrectly. What is your likely first reaction? Select one.
   (a) I should have done it myself. It would have been done the right way. ☐
   (b) I'll look in my own files first. It might have been my fault. ☐

(Continued)

(c) I should have explained what I wanted more carefully. □
(d) Perhaps someone else can find it. □

2. The most effective way to motivate your coworkers is by telling them:
   (a) You are not as interested in your work as you used to be. You must try harder. □
   (b) Please double-check with me if you are in doubt about the assignment. □
   (c) Don't change my instructions unless you are sure your approach is better. □
   (d) Try to do the job yourself; you can handle it, if you really want to. □

3. You just promoted one of your coworkers. Being interested in the reaction of others, you say, "It could not have happened to a nicer person, don't you agree?" Then you notice that this remark is being repeated to others by a particular employee. What is your most likely reaction?
   (a) The employee wants to be known as a nice person. □
   (b) The employee could be really jealous and trying to cover up real feelings. □
   (c) The employee wants to make friends with the coworker who was promoted. □
   (d) The employee feels that this promotion is good for the morale of the company. □

Scoring and Interpretation

1. (a) = 1   2. (a) = 1   3. (a) = 1
   (b) = 2   (b) = 3   (b) = 4
   (c) = 3   (c) = 2   (c) = 2
   (d) = 4   (d) = 4   (d) = 3

Compute your scores according to the values given in the above key.

A score of 9 to 12 shows that you are taking the right approach in bringing out the best in your companions. You don't just blame them, you instruct them.

A score of 6 to 8 reveals your readiness to delegate (at least theoretically), but deeper down you are afraid that the coworker might do a better job than you and endanger your position.

A score of 3 to 5 is a low score for a top manager. It might mean that you have a low opinion of your coworkers. You cannot communicate effectively.

Leadership involves many roles: planning, controlling, communicating, discipline, but, most of all, motivating. A top manager must have these three qualities:

1. Consistency and reliability (more about this later).
2. Courage—the ability to ask why. This may involve creating new approaches within the organization, developing new products, style or hiring different employees.
3. The ability to bring out the best in coworkers. This is perhaps the most important quality of a top manager. It is not a matter of manipulation, criticism, or random compliments, although all these play important roles. Most people will naturally gravitate toward the person who makes *them* feel good about themselves, the person who helps them grow and develop their own self-esteem. Real leaders first take into consideration the welfare and self-esteem of coworkers and do not flaunt their own egos.

A top manager will have to play psychologist. Understanding how to influence coworkers without merely exercising authority is important.

Here's What Could Have Happened

"I guess that's what was meant," the employee mutters while proceeding to execute the order. When the task is done, the boss blows up. "This isn't what I wanted!"

Who is at fault? Too often a supervisor or manager thinks what is required is perfectly obvious to everyone. There are several reasons why communication is unclear:

1. The person in charge may be impatient.
2. A supervisor may overestimate the ability of coworkers to understand and follow orders.
3. A boss may really want staff to fail to prove his or her superiority.
4. Sometimes orders are given in such a nebulous way as to invite misinterpretation (so as to make the boss indispensable?).
5. A manager is not sure how the job should be executed and secretly hopes for guidance from staff.

Consistency

Consistency is another quality required in a top manager. Many of us are confused and undecided about alternatives in business. Consistency eliminates needless thinking.

Skillful leaders try very hard to persuade their staffs to accept a decision. Once the followers have committed themselves to this decision, their subsequent actions will likely fall into line. For example, many people read advertisements praising a product *after* they have bought it. This convinces them that they made the right choice.

Once coworkers accept a statement and agree with it, other requests are complied with more easily. In other words, the "misery of choice" is eliminated. Dictators take advantage of this fact. Dictators (they exist in management as well as politics) try to perpetuate dependence while positive leaders train people to act independently.

What type of leader are you? Do you induce compliance via consistency? Try this test.

┌─ Test ────────────────────────────────

Select the one answer for each question that best expresses your feelings.

1. You read the following financial statements of various companies. In which one would you most likely invest?
   (*a*) We have increased our sales by 10 percent every year: in 1980, $1,865,000; in 1981–1982, $2,000,000; and in 1982, $2,103,000. ☐
   (*b*) We did all right. Our profits were 9 percent of volume in 1979, 10 percent in 1980, and 8 percent in 1981. ☐
   (*c*) We sold 5 percent more units every year. ☐
   (*d*) We have maintained our profit margin by averaging out over the last 3 years and have increased our volume in line with the population growth. ☐

2. As a business manager you made a statement about the number of failures in the fur business last year. Someone points out that this figure is wrong. What is your most likely reaction?
   (*a*) I try to correct my statement by citing a qualifying factor such as "I meant only exclusive or expensive fur stores." ☐
   (*b*) I admit my error and state that I must have mixed up my data. ☐
   (*c*) I try to defend my statement on the basis of my authority. ☐
   (*d*) I promise to bring proof and cite the source of my information (although I am not sure I really will). ☐

3. The new warehouse that a contractor built for you starts to develop cracks after only a few months. You are terribly upset. What do you do? (Choose one.)
   (*a*) I start a lawsuit against the contractor. The contract contained a clause to protect me against negligence. ☐

(b) I accept the blame for having bargained with the contractor too much, so that the company had to scrimp and save on materials. ☐
(c) I could not have foreseen that the land under the building had been a filled-in area. I'll just have to bring in cement pilings. ☐
(d) Luckily I provided for emergency shoring up. Thus the repair was not too costly. ☐

Scoring and Interpretation

1. (a) = 1   2. (a) = 3   3. (a) = 2
   (b) = 2   (b) = 4   (b) = 3
   (c) = 3   (c) = 1   (c) = 2
   (d) = 4   (d) = 2   (d) = 4

Compute your scores according to the values given in the above key.

The best score is 8 to 12. You are a leader; you look ahead.
A score of 5 to 7 puts you on the borderline.
A score of 3 to 4 shows that you jump in when it is almost too late.

A good leader can be relied upon to foresee the consequences of any action. Followers are reassured and provided with confidence. When a leader does have to reverse facts, an intelligent explanation is given.

Consistency can be learned. Make sure of as many facts as possible so that you can avoid unwitting contradictions. You have to realize that everything you say and do is scrutinized. Sometimes contradictory gestures can undermine people's confidence in you.

ASKING "WHY NOT?"— ANOTHER LEADERSHIP ROLE

The development of successful companies and new products and the saving of faltering businesses are often the result of someone in the top echelon asking, "Why not?"

Before we give away any more ideas, here is a test you can use to measure this leadership skill.

┌─ **Test** ───

Select the one answer for each question that best expresses your feelings.

1. You are in charge of developing new markets and applications for fluorescent lights. They are now used mostly in kitchens, offices, and stores. How can you get them to be used in other rooms? First, put down your ideas, then compare them to those listed.

   (*a*) Make a whole wall glow. It can be filled with the same gases as a fluorescent tube.
   (*b*) Combine fluorescent tubes and incandescent lights so that they may be elegant and usable for the living room.
   (*c*) Build small tubes into an electric typewriter to light up the area.
   (*d*) Use a small clip on a tube to light up telephones.

2. You manufacture and print road maps for motorists. Think of the new ways to make them more practical for use while the motorist is driving. First jot down your own ideas, and then compare them with ours.

   (*a*) Put the map on a scroll. As the trip progresses, the driver follows the map. The driver can move it sideways and so doesn't have to unfold a big, unwieldy map.
   (*b*) Put the maps on slides which can be projected next to the driver onto the window.
   (*c*) Mount large road maps on posters at street intersections. Rent part of the space to advertisers.
   (*d*) Project map via videocassette.

3. You help design a new-car model. You study the habits of modern motorists. What improvements are suggested by asking, Why not? Put down your ideas first, then compare them with our examples.

   (*a*) Create a better way of getting bags from the supermarket cart into the car. Maybe tracks can be pulled out of the car and the cart shoved from its underpinning on the tracks into the car.
   (*b*) Add telescopic luggage racks. Extend them like the radio antenna as high as needed for the luggage. When they are not used, they can be pushed back.

(c) Add a built-in chemical toilet on the floor of the car for use while traveling with small children.

(d) Add an opening in the floor where trash can be deposited temporarily, to be emptied later at a convenient spot, at home, or in a litter basket.

4. An office furniture manufacturer needs new ideas. Put down your own ideas first; then compare with ours.

(a) Turntable bookshelves, doubling the space for books or other storage.   ☐

(b) A panel on the desk which lights up labels of shelves when a button is pushed and facilitates finding stored items, books, etc.   ☐

(c) Movable desks which can, like a lectern, be put on a rack at various spots in the office, permitting a stand-up operation (which is healthier) and a change of position plus the convenience of taking notes.   ☐

Scoring and Interpretation

In this test, your leadership ability is judged by your answers and their comparison to our suggestions. Our examples are based on real situations. The leaders involved often brought a company back from disaster by having the courage to question established procedures.

They showed optimism and courage.

The more suggestions you could jot down, not necessarily similar to our cited case studies, the better you will be able to fill this leadership role.

A company producing trailers had the idea of promoting them as extra guest bedrooms. The trailer could be connected to the house for water and electricity; once the guests were gone, the trailer could be returned to its usual use. Why not?

We developed an approach which we called *operation daydream*. It can be applied to almost any kind of company. We did it for a paper company, asking what new products could be used—from the moment a person wakes up. The results were surprising.

Millions of people need to take medication during the night. In asking "Why not?" we came up with such ideas as dimly lit night tables and medication bottles with braille labels.

Using *crossover applications* or, more scientifically, *technological transfer* often produces very profitable and highly marketable new products and ideas.

Based on these principles, a thermometer was developed in the form of a small adhesive tape which changes color according to the temperature of the patient. It can be used once and discarded, eliminating hygienic complications.

Coworkers who are stimulated to concentrate on questions and even on well-established procedures find their jobs more challenging and interesting. Many companies have suggestion boxes where ideas can be received and the best ones are rewarded.

You, too, can be comfortable saying, "Why not?" Try setting up a library of unusual ideas. Use products reported in the press—these ideas may stimulate new ones. Try new approaches, demonstrate your ability to think differently. Teach your associates to do likewise. Take them on a safari—a trip into the unexplored jungle of the mind.

MOTIVATING YOURSELF AND OTHERS

What is the most important motivation in life? Good question. There is no simple answer. We tend to think of motivations as linear. They are, however, like cog wheels—they rotate at varying speeds, in different directions, meshing constantly with other cog wheels in infinite combinations.

We complain that a coworker is not motivated. Yet, that same person may be a whiz on the golf course. Our goals may be too high or too low. If they are not within reach, we are not motivated. In hiring or trying to stimulate an associate, it is important to ascertain his or her degree of motivation. How well do you motivate yourself and others?

Test

Select the one answer for each question that best expresses your feelings.

1. What are you doing about improving your physical well-being?
   (*a*) I exercise regularly. ☐
   (*b*) I follow a diet. ☐

(c) I am healthy. I don't need to do anything special. ☐
(d) I take vitamins, exercise and keep my weight down, and check my blood pressure. ☐

2. What are you doing to improve yourself?
   (a) I am learning a new language, new skills. ☐
   (b) I did enough studying to last me a lifetime. I can't use all the knowledge I have now. ☐
   (c) I prefer to pursue my hobbies. ☐
   (d) I have little time to do additional things; I read professional books. ☐

3. What are your relationships with your community or non-work-related organizations?
   (a) I am not a joiner; it is usually pointless. ☐
   (b) I am a member of several activity groups. ☐
   (c) I have actively started an organization or movement. ☐
   (d) I vote, or go to church, I belong to a club, but I leave politics and fighting for/or discussing social issues to others. ☐

4. An associate under your supervision has done a poor job. You have to choose among various methods to achieve better performance next time. What is your most likely method?
   (a) I point out how many mistakes were made. ☐
   (b) I don't mention the mistakes at all; I correct what was done wrong. ☐
   (c) I discuss why the mistakes were made. ☐
   (d) I say, "You must have been unclear about your instructions." ☐

5. You ask your staff to think of ways to improve sales and to present ideas at the next meeting. They don't come up with any new ideas. What is your most likely reaction?
   (a) My instructions were clear. They didn't listen well. ☐
   (b) It's my fault. I'll have to go over the assignment in greater detail to really excite them. ☐
   (c) My staff is not creative enough. I'll have to do it myself. ☐
   (d) I'll discuss cases of other sales people, talk about their difficulties at first and how they succeeded in the end. ☐

Scoring and Interpretation

1.	2.	3.	4.	5.
(a) = 4	(a) = 4	(a) = 1	(a) = 3	(a) = 1
(b) = 2	(b) = 1	(b) = 2	(b) = 4	(b) = 3
(c) = 1	(c) = 2	(c) = 4	(c) = 3	(c) = 2
(d) = 4	(d) = 3	(d) = 3	(d) = 4	(d) = 4

(Continued)

Compute your scores according to the values given in the above key.

A score of 15 to 20 is good. It shows that you consider your staff to be competent and that you know how to motivate them.
A score of 10 to 14 reveals a manager who is too eager to blame coworkers.
A score of 5 to 9 could reveal a manager who is too readily satisfied with the status quo. No need for improvement is required.

We learn right from wrong by continuous reward and punishment. B. F. Skinner, the behaviorist, claims that we are almost completely trainable and motivated through reinforcements. Freud stands at the opposite end, defending the importance of emotionality and irrationality of human drives.

As a practical manager, you don't have time for such academic disputes. You want to know: Are you properly motivated? How can you stimulate unmotivated colleagues?

Set a goal. There can be no motivation without a definite purpose. Thus, as simple as it may sound, the definition, and clear visualization of the final destination, is the key. If the goal is attractive enough, it will work as a motivator.

An employee without a goal to reach will not try very hard, if at all. Lack of motivation is accompanied by a feeling of futility, uselessness. A goal must be established, be it money, recognition, or a share in the company's success. Everyone needs an incentive.

Although goals may differ with each individual, as a manager, you can determine what excites your coworkers.

The following section offers some approaches for better understanding these motivating forces.

HOW GOOD AN EXAMPLE DO YOU SET?

The top manager is not automatically at the top. The organization as we know it today, in its hierarchical and centralized form, will begin to resemble real democracy, and the ability to motivate will become more important.

We can see beginnings of such changes: Management from the bottom up places the brunt of responsibility on the corporate president or chief executive officer (CEO). The clerk or low-level employee blames mishaps on the supervisor who is better trained (and better paid). And so it goes, up the corporate ladder.

To learn this new practice of blame reversal, experimental laboratories should be established. Instead of finding out what the secretary or the assistant did wrong, the manager must learn what went wrong in communications.

Some modern high schools have adopted this new approach and allow students who are bored to leave the classroom. The students can choose among three or four classes until they find the right ones. Evening seminars are held to help less experienced teachers improve their teaching techniques.

Interpersonal relations can be measured. How well liked are you? How many relationships do you have with your peers? How many would you like to have? If you can see yourself through the eyes of your coworkers, you can change your habits.

Leadership positions are being considered more often for those who can establish a feeling of partnership with the "troops." It is desirable to sympathize, to help with coworkers' problems, to protect rather than dictate. A good leader sets a good example.

Acculturation

We are becoming aware that each organization is a culture in itself. A new employee must learn to overcome "culture shock." Yes, it's true—a newcomer must adapt to the customs and rituals of the corporate rules. Perhaps companies should hand out a booklet listing rules and desired modes of behavior as well as a credo or description of the company culture and its origin. And an older and more experienced person could act as social director to help novices over all the initial hurdles. After all, a new job is like a cruise ship—it takes a while to feel at home.

CHANGING THOUGHT MODELS

The average person usually describes progress as a straight ascending line. When we talk about human needs, we think of a pie chart. In both cases, we reveal the models that underlie our thinking processes. In both cases, however, the model utilized is erroneous. Before we tell you more, what are your thought models? Take this test and see.

┌─ **Test** ─────────────────────────────

Select the one answer for each question that best expresses your feelings.

1. Why did mutual funds suffer reverses?
   (*a*) They were mismanaged. ☐
   (*b*) They grew too big. ☐
   (*c*) Other, more profitable investment opportunities developed. ☐
   (*d*) The stock market went into a decline. ☐

2. This is the real reason why some large publications went under:
   (*a*) Their staffs had become too expensive. ☐
   (*b*) Readers wanted more up-to-date news coverage. ☐
   (*c*) The price for each copy had become too high. ☐
   (*d*) Readers wanted more individual-oriented publications. ☐

3. Job applicants who blow their own horns usually
   (*a*) Have a good reason. ☐
   (*b*) Are covering up insufficiencies. ☐
   (*c*) Are trying to sell themselves. ☐
   (*d*) Feel it is expected. ☐

4. You are about to be transferred to another branch overseas. Which would you be most likely to do to prepare yourself?
   (*a*) Interview some people who worked in this branch and returned. ☐
   (*b*) Go on a test visit for a few weeks. ☐
   (*c*) Ask a colleague who is there what the possibilities are. ☐
   (*d*) Discard information not based on my own experience. ☐

Scoring and Interpretation

1.		2.		3.		4.	
(*a*)	=1	(*a*)	=1	(*a*)	=2	(*a*)	=1
(*b*)	=4	(*b*)	=3	(*b*)	=3	(*b*)	=3
(*c*)	=2	(*c*)	=2	(*c*)	=4	(*c*)	=2
(*d*)	=3	(*d*)	=4	(*d*)	=1	(*d*)	=4

Compute your scores according to the values given in the above key.

Here are our reasons for the scoring:
The highest score is from 14 to 16. This manager is aware of the influence of thought models and structures, their value, and their danger.
In item 1, (*b*) is the best answer. When they handled very large numbers of investors, mutual funds became unmanageable. They could not move and change their investments rapidly enough.

In item 2, (d) is the best answer. *Life, Look, Saturday Evening Post,* and other publications had lost sight of the fact that readers wanted more individualized news. Smaller and more specialized publications took over. Had the publishers of the large publications been aware of their wrong thought structures, they could have avoided failure.

In item 3, (c) is right. Item 3(b) represents an oversimplified attempt at a pseudopsychological explanation.

In item 4, (d) is the best answer. The approach in item 4(a) could be misleading because possibly only failures returned. Before emigrating to the United States, I made a mistake. I talked to people who had returned to Europe and heard only negative comments; then I realized that I had inadvertently selected a biased sample.

A score of 9 to 13 usually reflects a mixture of correct and incorrect thought models and structures.

A low score of 4 to 8 implies wrong thinking about human motivations.

Human progress is more correctly described as an ascending spiral. We come back to where we have been, but on a higher level.

Human needs should be portrayed as an expanding balloon rather than as slices of a pie. We tend to cut larger slices of the pie of life and, therefore, then think we just have fewer needs left. On the contrary, the appetite comes with eating, increasing the desire for satisfaction. Our language and thinking patterns are filled with such wrong static graphic models.

When these models are correct (in line with the real world and its structure), they can act as excellent guides. However, when we use an erroneous model, we think we're proceeding logically, but sooner or later we discover a maladjustment. As a motivational technique for changing human nature, we must make the individual aware of the model being used and then check these assumptions for correctness.

For a long time, the frozen food industry suffered because the consumer considered *frozen* to be the opposite of *fresh.* In a motivational research study, we found that such thinking existed and suggested it be changed by facts—those which showed that most "fresh" fruits and vegetables, upon reaching the market, were at least 3 to 4 days old on average. On the other hand, frozen foods were picked at the apex of ripeness, and the freezing was done immediately afterward. According to this model, frozen is really fresher than fresh.

What are your thought models? How can structures be developed, corrected, and checked? During a discussion, as a good exercise, stop for a moment and determine whether you have used a graphic design to organize your thoughts. You may find a triangle, square, or circle has popped up in your head to illustrate graphically an abstract idea and to make it more understandable.

Computerization, introduction of new technology, will result in the elimination of such jobs as those of telephone operators and perhaps even mail carriers. So waiting for unemployment to be reduced as a result of modern technology is wrong motivational thinking.

When hiring, a manager should assess both the previous experience and the adaptability of the applicant to another activity within the organization. The rapid change in today's economy and technologies may require equally rapid internal shifting.

In our schools, we train children to select from several different occupations, not just focus on one. *Retraining* is the new buzzword, but we have had little psychological preparation for it. There are no multioccupational unions yet, and there are few (if any) advertisements asking for managers or supervisors with "universal" abilities.

Instead, we still believe in the desirability of sharp job definitions. A person's capacity to shift, to change, to turn around will be valued in the future.

Market research and public opinion research still operate within the classic, often irrelevant, subdivisions of age, income, marital status, etc. We are only beginning to see that the important thing is whether your income is going up, standing still, or going down. The psychological segmentation of markets and the introduction of psychological typologies are fairly recent phenomena.

These dynamic categories represent only the replacement of wrong models with correct ones—correct in the sense of being instrumental and motivational rather than purely phenomenologically descriptive.

WAYS TO HEIGHTEN MOTIVATIONAL SKILLS

How can executives learn to be better motivators? Management grows more complex every day and involves more information handling, bigger risks, entry into new and unfamiliar product areas, heavier demands on available time, and a need for more effective communication, not only to customers but also to levels above and below within the corporation.

Most training methods haven't kept pace with the needs of modern executives. Typically, "canned" approaches attempt to fit the dynamic individual into present rules for performance. Moreover, most management training is hardly as sophisticated as the executives it attempts to teach, and thus it can't reach the prime management problems of improving decision making, creativity, and communications.

Proper motivation involves the following:

1. *Self-knowledge.* Initial sessions can encourage individuals to make a fresh recognition of their own abilities and weaknesses—how these abilities are changing and how they influence both mobility within the firm and relationships with peers.

2. *Information handling and control of the environment.* All modern executives must grapple with masses of computer-generated and other information and, at the same time, sharpen their perceptions of various markets and of their own business associates. Top managers should suggest solutions to such problems as how to approach and "personally" research totally unfamiliar business areas, how to sharpen observations of changes in the world, and how to benefit from new methods of storing and retrieving data. The present filing system is static. Top managers must teach a more dynamic and immediately usable form of information handling. Information should be not only readily accessible but also helpful in generating and defending unusual approaches.

3. *Personal organization.* The higher up an executive moves in an organization, the less time is available to her or him, so the more isolated a manager she or he will become. Telephone calls, meetings, business travel, and ceremonial functions are all time-consuming. The top manager can easily live out of sync with reality. New techniques are needed to help the executive determine priorities, classify information in functional rather than superficial ways, and organize an increasing workload.

4. *Dynamic technical communication.* Modern executives are still communicating with peer groups, superiors, subordinates, and outside business associates in outmoded ways. Do letters still have to exist in letter form? Is it possible to streamline internal communications—to develop new electronic devices that will allow for less tie-up of valuable executive time and will create a feeling of participation?

5. *Interpersonal relations.* Many executives and salespeople can gain by developing greater sensitivity in interpersonal relations. Too many people are passive rather than active listeners, can be tricked by superficial signals into making rash judgments, and don't utilize all their senses in observing people and things. Interpersonal relations can also be improved if the individual is confident, is not trying to play a role, and comes across as a genuine person.

6. *More creative thinking.* The modern executive has to make decisions, think problems through, and understand more and more

complex issues. But intelligent decisions are frequently blocked by misinterpreting other people's explanations and rationalizations, generalizing and attaching a label owing to a lack of proper information (or, frequently, a failure to ask insightful questions), getting trapped between two alternatives, and prejudice.

Also, it is becoming increasingly important for modern executives to develop new ideas, which they often feel inhibited about doing because of fear of change, rules of what can and can't be done, and concern about personal censorship. A new methodology has to be developed to free the individual in decision making and generating new ideas.

Too much of an executive's valuable time is controlled by convention: the way the desk is organized, the manner in which memoranda are written and distributed, supposed requirements for "selling" distributors and consumers, the products and outlets appropriate for the firm, the meetings, and the way the secretary keeps the files. Moreover, executives frequently don't have the time or skills to absorb things quickly enough—from their daily papers to their superior's speech and expressions. New strategies are needed in dealing with both people and facts.

7. *Most importantly, encouragement to grow.*   Normally we operate only at 40 to 50 percent of our capacity. Being told and cajoled to utilize the other half of our potential is one of the most effective ways of motivating ourselves and others.

TEAMWORK
A HOT MANAGER'S
BEST TOOL

BEING A HOT MANAGER MEANS BEING A GOOD PARENT

Your coworkers look on you much as a parent. Many of the relationships are similar. You can punish and reward.

In a recent book entitled *Business Conferences*, written for a Soviet management organization, the author, Boris N. Volgin, emphasized that essential elements in a good meeting were humor and the ability for everyone to express opinions openly without fear of ridicule.[1] That is quite a step forward.

Try this test to find out how good a facilitator, parent, or teammate you and your colleagues are.

Test

Select the one answer for each question that best expresses your feelings.

1. A new idea has been presented by a member of the team. It resembles one that you were about to mention but didn't have the confidence to bring out in the open. Judging from previous incidents, what are you most likely to remark?

(Continued)

---

[1] Reported in an article entitled "Russians See a Funny Side to Business" by Theodore Sahabad, *The New York Times*, August 14, 1983, Section 1, page 11.

(*a*) "That's interesting. I was just about to mention a very similar idea." ☐

(*b*) "It's a good idea, but it can't be executed as it has been presented. It needs a lot of work yet and must be thought through." ☐

(*c*) I keep silent about my own similar idea and congratulate whoever presented it. ☐

(*d*) I encourage the group to acknowledge the idea, but I come up with additional suggestions—possibly even contradictory ones. ☐

2. Everybody is participating in the discussion except one colleague, who keeps quiet. What is your most likely reaction to the person's silence?

(*a*) It's best to leave the situation alone. Not everyone is vocal. ☐

(*b*) I ask a question directly, to draw the person out. ☐

(*c*) I joke about his or her silence. For instance, I might say, "So-and-so doesn't want to give away any great ideas." ☐

(*d*) I tell my colleague that ideas are valuable, even if they sound crazy at first. ☐

3. You are in charge of making seating arrangements in the conference room for the next meeting. The windows are very bright and glaring. The corner seat is subject to through traffic. Analyze your motivations. Which one honestly applies to you most of the time?

(*a*) I make sure that I sit with my back to the glaring windows. ☐

(*b*) I secretly detest Bill. I assign the seat facing the windows or the corner seat to him. ☐

(*c*) Jovita is new and somewhat shy. I will assign the most comfortable seat to her. ☐

(*d*) Frank and Shirley always support my ideas. I shall seat them to my left and right. ☐

4. You are uncomfortable because one participant is constantly interrupting everybody else to push forth ideas. How should this be handled? One answer please!

(*a*) Tell the coworker to shut up and let the others talk. ☐

(*b*) Use the coworker's ideas and challenge others to destroy or accept them. ☐

(*c*) Ask the disturber to develop the ideas further. ☐

(*d*) Limit talking time for everybody. ☐

5. What is the best way to compose a team? Choose one answer.

(*a*) Invite people with similar interests and from the same department. ☐

(*b*) Invite people from completely different fields and other sections of the company. ☐

(*c*) Put antagonists together, conservatives, innovators, pushy people, dreamers, and realists. ☐

(d) Split the team into technical people, salespeople, and organizational, long-range planners. ☐

6. You are to compose a team to solve a company's problem. You can select only five people, not including yourself. Which five will you include?
   (a) A technical person who is an expert in the field. ☐
   (b) A production expert who knows how to work things out properly. ☐
   (c) A person who knows the competition and the marketplace. ☐
   (d) A creative person. ☐
   (e) Someone who has expressed doubts about the whole operation and does not believe that the company should be involved in this project. ☐
   (f) The accountant of the company. ☐
   (g) The company lawyer. ☐
   (h) A computer and data specialist. ☐

7. The company you work for intends to open an office abroad. A memorandum is being circulated asking for people to participate in a meeting relating to this new foreign office. What is your most likely reaction to this invitation?
   (a) I would have nothing to contribute. I am not interested in moving. ☐
   (b) I'll go to the meeting. Who knows, maybe it will be an interesting opportunity. ☐
   (c) Even though I would not be interested in moving, I think I have good ideas to contribute. ☐
   (d) There will be a lot of talk, and nothing will come of it. If I am asked specifically, I'll go, but reluctantly. ☐
   (e) I wonder who else is going to the meeting. I'll inquire first, before I decide whether to go. ☐

Scoring and Interpretation

1. $(a) = 1$ 2. $(a) = 2$ 3. $(a) = 1$ 4. $(a) = 1$ 5. $(a) = 1$
   $(b) = 3$ $(b) = 3$ $(b) = 2$ $(b) = 4$ $(b) = 3$
   $(c) = 4$ $(c) = 1$ $(c) = 4$ $(c) = 3$ $(c) = 4$
   $(d) = 2$ $(d) = 4$ $(d) = 3$ $(d) = 2$ $(d) = 2$

6. $(a), (b), (c), (d), (e) = 4$; $(c), (d), (e), (g), (h) = 3$; $(a), (b), (c), (e), (f) = 2$

(Continued)

7. $(a) = 1$
   $(b) = 5$
   $(c) = 4$
   $(d) = 2$
   $(e) = 3$

Compute your scores according to the values given in the above key.

Items 1, 3, 6, and 7 measure your qualifications as a teammate. The highest score is 17 for these four items.

Items 2, 4, and 5 refer to your approach as a facilitator. For these the highest score is 12.

We combined the scores in order to make the test less obvious. You can then separate the two groups to arrive at a separate score for each faculty. The total highest score is 29; the total lowest score is 8.

Thus a score between 22 and 29 shows excellent abilities as a teammate and facilitator, abilities which overlap.

A lower score, between 15 and 21 depending on its composition, is frequently attained. We attribute higher scores to managers who chose more controversial participants and more creative people to work in a team.

Also, paying more attention to getting shy and new people to participate and to be less interested in personal comfort in arranging meetings deserved a better score.

Volgin's book also states, "Many meetings give the appearance of intense activity when, in fact, nothing happens." And he says, "A conference is a search for an optimum solution." The conclusion to be drawn is that the more that conflicting ideas are exposed and resolved, the more successful a meeting is going to be. Whether someone makes a good teammate depends on the person's ability to disagree, to express opinions, and create the very opposite of what we normally understand to be good team playing.

A team leader or team facilitator makes sure that enough friction is created to produce the sparks that make for a productive meeting. Teamwork, in a manual sense, means that everybody is pulling in the same direction. An intellectual team engages in a brainstorming session, with the emphasis on the word *storm*.

High-speed management is required to cope with rapidly changing consumer demands and obsolescence of products. As was pointed out in *Fortune* magazine,[2] the team of tomorrow must learn to live with

---

[2] Susan Fraker, "High Speed Management," *Fortune*, March 5, 1984, pp. 62–68.

disorder. A successful teammate and facilitator will be a person capable of creating friction.

Try inviting consumers and end users to participate in your boardroom and team meetings. They can set you straight about their wishes!

HOW BIG IS YOUR HALO?

Top executives are urged to compliment their colleagues as often as possible, but they, too, crave recognition and praise.

Some leaders want to be feared and respected. Being a tough boss can get you a good reputation for straightening out messes. Being admired is something between love and fear. You can buy love from your coworkers, but unless it's given voluntarily, it doesn't mean much. Where on the scale do you stand? Take this test before we say more.

Test

Select the one answer for each question that best expresses your feelings.

1. Think of the following animals: ant, beaver, lion, fox, elephant, eagle, mole, horse, dog, chameleon, spider, cat, mouse, albatross. If you were one of these, which would you be most like?
   (*a*) Choose the one animal most like yourself.

   (*b*) Now choose one animal, but this time guess what animal your coworkers would think most like you. In other words, if you see yourself as an eagle, would your coworkers agree or disagree with you? Repeat this step several times, asking several different people.

   (*c*) Now see how many times your own judgment and the assumed judgment of your peers coincided—1, 2, 3, 4, 5, 6, 7, or more times.

2. Your office workers are trying to organize a party. Of the first five people invited, which do you think you would be?
   (*a*) First choice ☐
   (*b*) Second choice ☐

(Continued)

(c) Third choice ☐
(d) Fourth choice ☐
(e) Fifth choice ☐

3. You found the following secret evaluation sheet about various employees. Which applies to you most?
   (a) Very aggressive, wants to get ahead at all costs, valuable for the organization but rather a loner. ☐
   (b) Seems to know everybody and gets along well with peers. Sometimes too much people-oriented rather than performance-oriented. ☐
   (c) Moody, can be charming, but often turns on you quite unexpectedly. Does the work satisfactorily but rather routinely. ☐

4. You get yourself in trouble by speaking ill of a colleague, who hears about it and confronts you. How would your other colleagues react?
   (a) Most would bawl me out. ☐
   (b) Two or three would go out of their way to defend me. ☐
   (c) Most continue to be superficially friendly, but keep their distance. ☐

Scoring and Interpretation

1. If your own judgment and that of your peers, according to your guess, coincide 1 to 3 times, your score is 3; if 4 to 5 times, your score is 2; and if 6 or more times, your score is 1. If the animals are usually portrayed in a flattering way, like the beaver, fox, lion, and eagle, add 1 point to your score.

2. (a), (b) = 3   3. (a) = 1   4. (a) = 2
   (c), (d) = 2   (b) = 3   (b) = 3
   (e) = 1   (c) = 2   (c) = 1

Compute your scores according to the values given in the above key.

The highest score for being liked is 10 to 13. You are considered a nice person and probably a good boss. A medium score is 7 to 9. You may be respected, but you are not necessarily liked.

A score of 4 to 6 indicates that the person tested, either yourself or a coworker, does not care to be well liked and puts more effort in getting things done, even at the expense of being considered tough.

The best overall tendency is to go in the direction of being a friend and taking care of your coworkers. Even in the army a good officer is one who is respected and liked at the same time.

We would all like to peek into a psychological mirror and know what others think of us. A *tough boss* is often just testing the staff, is afraid of getting involved and showing softness, like the sabra, the Israeli fruit which is hard on the outside but soft on the inside. Behind the tough exterior there is often a subconscious desire to be loved or liked. As a result of our macho culture, men in particular are afraid to appear mushy. A statement such as "I don't care if they all hate me as long as they do their jobs" reveals too protesting a tone to ring true.

A manager, like a parent, can be *liked or feared*. We should distinguish between authority and lack of it. A boss can be loved and still have authority. In fact, authority arising from affection may be more real than authority stemming from fear. It is more productive for all concerned to obey in order to please, rather than because of a fear of punishment.

Top managers are not unlike salespeople who must convince first themselves and then others to put themselves out for the company. According to the *Book of World Records*,[3] Mr. Girard is the most successful car salesman in the world. How does he explain his success? "I make people like me." Being liked is a better form of protection than being hated.

Most people prefer to be liked because it ensures that they will be involved in a process of *reciprocity*. Hardly anyone sets out deliberately to be disliked.

Managers don't have to be charming and smiling all the time, but colleagues do appreciate concern for their problems. The positive relationship works in both directions. We often overlook that the manager, too, wants to be complimented every so often for having done a good job.

Remembering birthdays and anniversaires, inquiring about someone's health, or making an occasional personal contact can be practiced daily and such gestures are usually handsomely rewarded.

ARE YOU SURROUNDED BY "IDIOTS"?

We make fun of them. We envy them. They seem to have permanence and security. And yet, in a study for a Canadian union (The Public Service Alliance), we found that the public servants themselves did not feel very secure in their jobs. With every change of government, they could be dismissed.

---

[3] Norris McWhirter, *Guinness Book of World Records*, Sterling, New York, 1985.

These questions were designed to dig beneath the surface and find out which people are best suited to routine bureaucratic jobs and which could be encouraged to grow.

Test

Select the one answer for each question that best expresses your feelings.

1. You manage an insurance company. You suggest that the employees attend a course on ethics given by a philosophy professor. What, in your estimation, will be the reaction of most of your people?
    (*a*) This is a crazy idea. We have better things to do. ☐
    (*b*) If we don't go, it will be held against us. ☐
    (*c*) It will kill time; let's hope it is on company time. ☐
    (*d*) This is an excellent idea. We should always learn something new. ☐

2. In Europe, a young woman bought a motorbike. She wanted to take it along on a Mediterranean trip but needed the signature of the dealer. She was sent from one government office to another. Finally someone said "Idiot, why don't you sign it yourself?" So she did. What is your most likely reaction?
    (*a*) It's illegal. Suppose everybody did it! ☐
    (*b*) Finally, someone with independence! ☐
    (*c*) We need more people like that who can break routines. ☐
    (*d*) It's OK, but how often do you find someone like that? It could create chaos if everyone acted similarly. ☐

3. You receive a complaint about an employee who went over the head of his superior. Your response is that the act might have been justified, but . . .
    (*a*) We'd have chaos if this became a regular practice. ☐
    (*b*) Regular channels should have been tried first, although perhaps this was the only course of action available. ☐
    (*c*) Rules should be established so that workers could pass on negative observations with impunity. ☐
    (*d*) This person has guts and should be promoted. ☐

4. You are giving an instruction to a coworker to change some of the procedures for filling an order. To which situation do you react most favorably?
    (*a*) The coworker insists that you give the order in writing. ☐
    (*b*) The coworker demands an exact, step-by-step description of the change. ☐
    (*c*) The coworker compliments you on this change. ☐
    (*d*) The coworker suggests new ideas to add to your instruction. ☐

5. You come back from a long trip. One of your associates took the initiative and rearranged office procedures. What is your most likely reaction?
   (*a*) I am glad about the change. ☐
   (*b*) I am angry at not being consulted first. ☐
   (*c*) I am jealous and hurt. ☐
   (*d*) I accept the changes with minor adjustments. ☐

Scoring and Interpretation

1.	(*a*) = 1	2.	(*a*) = 1	3.	(*a*) = 1	4.	(*a*) = 1	5.	(*a*) = 4
	(*b*) = 2		(*b*) = 3		(*b*) = 2		(*b*) = 2		(*b*) = 1
	(*c*) = 3		(*c*) = 4		(*c*) = 3		(*c*) = 3		(*c*) = 2
	(*d*) = 4		(*d*) = 2		(*d*) = 4		(*d*) = 4		(*d*) = 3

Compute your scores according to the values given in the above key.

Almost everybody is against bureaucrats. They are synonymous with inefficiency. Yet managers, even good ones, often surround themselves with bureaucrats. It gives managers the feeling of control because everything is being done according to the rules. At first, this seems like an efficient way to avoid disorder and conflicting views.

If you scored between 16 and 20, you give your staff sufficient freedom.

A score between 10 and 15 shows that you often create your own bureaucracy, even though you may call it discipline.

A score of 5 to 9 shows you to be a dictator. Your orders have to be followed; otherwise, you feel threatened.

Many private companies employ or breed bureaucrats without realizing it. While bureaucracy may have a place in government, although even that can be disputed, it certainly contradicts everything we know about good modern management.

If your score is low, you must train yourself to delegate more—not just as a thoughtless, repeated practice but as a real habit.

What bothers people who are ambitious is that promotions are often awarded according to time on the job rather than the worker's ability. Public servants don't like to feel they are merely serving the public. They want to feel important—that they are doing a job no one else would (or could).

Even in private enterprise, we need bureaucrats, or people to do the routine jobs. Contrary to popular misconceptions, these jobs *can* be rewarding. Bureaucrats can think about other problems while working. However, bureaucrats can be dangerous obstacles to progress. They have a basic fear of assuming responsibility and being incapable of doing the job.

Let us suggest one idea that worked for the Jewel Tea Company in Chicago. Right after being hired, many employees were set adrift. Within a broad outline of duties, they had to find their own direction and reach of activities. Almost half the new staff, usually coming directly from rigidly circumscribed work definitions, could not handle the freedom and left.

Independence within a large organization seems contradictory. Yet, this is exactly what free enterprise implies. It is a new type of democratic discipline, rather than one dictated by a hierarchy. But such freedom must be learned. Companies are being put through a reeducation process. Management will face similar rethinking with the next generation of top managers.

HOW MORAL ARE YOUR COWORKERS?

Why should ethics and morality enter into the employee evaluation process? As long as employees perform well, that should be sufficient. However, through a study we discovered that employees' performance was profoundly influenced by their knowledge that they worked for a company with a moral conviction. At the other extreme, absenteeism, cheating (in various forms), and drinking were all condoned and rationalized as a quid pro quo. These employees say, "If the company has no qualms about merchandising shoddy products and overcharging, why should we be so righteous?"

How do you assess the moral ethics of a potential colleague? What repercussions will follow? Take the following test. Be honest. No one will see the answers but you.

┌─ Test ─────────────────────────────────

Select the one answer for each question that best expresses your feelings.

1. You hear that an executive of an airline can put airline employees in first class even though they pay only for economy class. This executive offers to list you as an employee so you can benefit from this arrangement. What do you say?

(a) It is only a fair business deal. I have been giving a lot of business to this airline. ☐

(b) Sooner or later this is going to result in a disclosure. I do not want to be involved. ☐

(c) I appreciate this offer but decline. ☐

(d) It's a good deal. I try to take advantage of it as often as possible. Why not? ☐

2. A colleague tells you that the company permits the sale of a defective product. The public, they claim, will never know. With which one of your colleague's statements would you agree?

(a) I should blow the whistle and denounce the company to the respective authorities. Their practice is dangerous and highly unethical. ☐

(b) I am not going to risk my job. Sooner or later the buyer will find out. ☐

(c) I will send an anonymous letter to my supervisor, mentioning the unethical attitude. ☐

(d) I will demonstrate how easily the defect can be remedied without a loss to the company. ☐

3. A manager working for a vitamin company tells you that many vitamins have great value but others have no merit at all. What advice do you give?

(a) Collect expert opinions and send them to the top officials. ☐

(b) Send an anonymous memorandum to the press to relieve the guilt feelings. ☐

(c) Try to convince the company to sell only "good" vitamins, to drop those that are a fad, and to present this view in their advertisements. ☐

(d) If the public is gullible, too bad. Why should you stick your neck out? ☐

4. A salesperson offers to pay you a commission under the table if you recommend a particular product. The product is good, so no harm is being done. What is your most likely reaction?

(a) It's common business practice. I have to be competitive. ☐

(b) I prefer to share my knowledge; often a buyer has no experience with techniques involved. ☐

(c) I reject any bribe to promote a product. ☐

(d) I offer a legitimate discount in line with the competition. ☐

5. Your company has financial difficulties which, if known, would influence the stock value considerably. What would most managers do?

(a) Issue a statement that a new loan was being negotiated to cover increased production expenditures, due to increased sales. ☐

(Continued)

(*b*) Explain that it is only a bookkeeping problem. □
(*c*) Drive up the stock through announcements of forthcoming new products and then sell part of the portfolio to reap a profit. □
(*d*) Admit part of the truth, but explain it as a temporary failure in production schedule. □

Scoring and Interpretation

1. (*a*) = 2	2. (*a*) = 4	3. (*a*) = 4	4. (*a*) = 1	5. (*a*) = 3
(*b*) = 4	(*b*) = 1	(*b*) = 3	(*b*) = 2	(*b*) = 2
(*c*) = 3	(*c*) = 2	(*c*) = 2	(*c*) = 4	(*c*) = 1
(*d*) = 1	(*d*) = 3	(*d*) = 1	(*d*) = 3	(*d*) = 4

Compute your scores according to the values given in the above key.

The highest score is 20, the lowest 5.

Thus if your score is between 16 and 20, assuming you told us and yourself the truth, you or your associates are moral in your business behavior.

A score between 11 and 15 shows your belief that in many circumstances your peers would not hesitate to behave unethically.

A low score of 5 to 10 begins to reflect upon you as well as your colleagues.

We have deliberately concentrated on asking about your reactions to other people's behavior, thus leaving doubts about your own attitudes. It is a classic example of a *projective technique*. It was originally developed by Professor H. Murray, a psychologist at Harvard. He showed his subjects illustrations and asked for their interpretations. A famous example of this thematic apperception test is the case of a child peeping through a keyhole. You are being asked what the child sees. Of course, you can't tell, but your answers reveal a lot about you.

We found that few people are 100 percent ethical. In our pretest many more people chose a compromise answer, such as 1(*d*) (25 percent) and 1(*c*) (50 percent) or 4(a) (30 percent).

Insurance companies rank lowest in reputation for reliability and integrity. There are hundreds of thousands of people who feel that they have a perfect right to overstate a claim because they have been taken advantage of by an insurance company.

Unions often feel that working for a liquor or pharmaceutical firm which has been indicted for unethical practices entitles them to silent blackmail.

In hiring a new associate, you would put more credence in someone who admits to an ethical attitude, combined with realism. If all answers point to a flawless morality, that person is probably kidding you—and even worse, himself or herself.

Can you train people to become moral? Probably not. Only a small number of people obey all, or even some, of the Ten Commandments. Punishment, including the threat of hell, has not been very effective. Thus, for management's sake, an indirect form of morality is preferable. Admit your fallibility. Such honesty produces better teamwork and understanding.

WHAT IS THE INNER IMAGE OF YOUR COMPANY?

In a large computer company, we wanted to find out what the employees really felt about the company. Most corporations are aware of the importance of their "outer" image, but few are concerned with how their staff reacts.

This test was designed to test the degree and type of "inner image" that employees have about their place of work. A manager should be aware of the real corporate image, in order to take any action deemed necessary and to ensure the cooperation of various members of the industrial complex.

--- Test ---

Select the one answer for each question that best expresses your feelings.

1. If the leftmost square represents your company, which size would you be?

Company   You

(a) ☐   (b) ☐   (c) ☐

2. In your mind, on what kind of road is your company traveling?
(a) ☐   (b) ☐   (c) ☐   (d) ☐

(Continued)

3.. Which represents the appreciation you feel from your superiors or coworkers?
    (*a*) Cold shower. ☐
    (*b*) Bouquet of flowers. ☐
    (*c*) Pat on shoulder. ☐
    (*d*) Embrace. ☐

4. What do you think of your coworkers?
    (*a*) Most are wearing a mask, disguising their real feelings. ☐
    (*b*) Most are honest and behave as real people. ☐
    (*c*) Usually they are out to blame someone else. ☐
    (*d*) They accept their responsibilities, and I accept mine. ☐

5. If you became sick or disabled, how long would your colleagues and coworkers stick by you?
    (*a*) They would try to replace me after a "decent" time. ☐
    (*b*) They would put me on an easier job. ☐
    (*c*) They would keep me longer than necessary. ☐

Scoring and Interpretation

1.	2.	3.	4.	5.
(*a*) = 1	(*a*) = 1	(*a*) = 1	(*a*) = 1	(*a*) = 1
(*b*) = 3	(*b*) = 2	(*b*) = 2	(*b*) = 3	(*b*) = 2
(*c*) = 2	(*c*) = 3	(*c*) = 3	(*c*) = 2	(*c*) = 3
	(*d*) = 4	(*d*) = 4	(*d*) = 4	

Compute your scores according to the values given in the above key.

The best score is between 13 and 18. The inner image of your company is excellent. You feel you are being appreciated. Sometimes, as in item 1, you are bigger than your organization.

A score of 9 to 12 classifies you with most employees that we have tested.

The lowest score, 5 to 8, though acceptable in the average worker is probably a danger sign in executives or their peers. It would be advisable to find out why such feelings of frustration exist and then to seek remedies.

Clearly, if the employees of a company are not fully convinced about its worth, from a moral or business viewpoint, then they can't be very enthusiastic about it to outsiders. However, it will not do to ask the employees directly. In a survey for General Motors, a Cadillac was promised for the best explanation of why General Motors was a good place to work. As expected, many answered so as to ensure winning. We were asked to try an in-depth approach. Workers were asked what they appreciated most *and* what they liked least. We developed a "voltmeter." The greater the distance between the positive and negative values of needle spread, the more important we judged the item to be. In the previous survey, the most frequent answer was "Working for a large company." In our test, we received answers such as "Shoeshine machines are appreciated." Special soap to get motor oil and chemicals off the hands was sorely missed. In other words, the inner image of the company was based on emotional and personal demonstrations of consideration at the *human level.*

Not enough top managers are aware of the importance of primary customers' (employees') feelings about the organization. Staying close within the company is as important as staying close to the customer.

Sometimes it is helpful for top managers to have rewards built into the daily routine, e.g., to break up the routine with minor celebrations. Today's offices should offer enrichment, from plants to favorite books and hobbies. Will future specialists find that a top manager who does not permit relaxation during the workday builds stress? It seems unreasonable to work 7 to 10 hours and wait until evening to unwind. Relaxation, just like physical exercise, should be taken in small, regular doses.

Some companies would do well to have special offices reserved for human "nonwork" contact. Teamwork should not be reserved only for designated hours and meetings. Why not have a continuous discussion room where anyone could drop in and be heard? Think about it.

TEAMWORK—HOW TO IMPROVE IT

Group decisions are neither work nor cooperation. Group decisions combine the intelligence and viewpoints of different people. To call them committee decisions invites ridicule. The idea is to bring together knowledgeable people, not necessarily to reach agreement but rather to permit each person to see the same problem from different corporate viewpoints.

Synectics is a term used to describe this multiprofessional approach. With this method, a technical problem may be handled by as varied a group as one composed of engineers, artists, salespeople, medical professionals, and tradespeople. Each person and occupation has its own set of psychological tools with which to approach a problem.

A plumber thinks in terms of pipes, valves, and pumps. A cardiologist uses almost identical concepts. Out of such brainstorming evolved a new *balloon technique* to clean out arteries which is similar to the Roto-Rooter approach. Basically, a catheter is inserted into the circulatory system, and the plaque which has collected in the pipes is reamed out.

A team works best if many different coworkers are placed together. The greater the controversy, the more fruitful the result can be. The more cooperation and sycophant attitudes there are, the more a team resembles a rubber stamp committee.

A top manager must learn to create dissension and to demand input. Theatrics is excellent training for a team moderator. Even going to a drama school may be good for a beginner. A team is a show: it needs orchestration and is based on conflicts and catharses. The emphasis should be on learning to master the methodology of finding answers. It might even be desirable to conduct special groups for the purpose of perfecting the techniques of forcing ideas, objections, and intelligent planning to the surface. At present, too much effort is put into finding answers instead of perfecting answer-finding methods.

A team should be organized so that the whole is greater than the sum of the parts. The moderator or facilitator should try to get the best out of the participants, as either antagonists or collaborators. In our seminars we choose an observer who later runs a special session in which contributions of each member are analyzed.

COMMUNICATION
A HOT MANAGER'S
MOST REVERED ATTRIBUTE

HOW WELL DO YOU KNOW YOUR
COWORKERS—AND SHOULD YOU?

Most new books on management stress the desirability of knowing personnel as well as possible. These books say it is a valuable trait for the top manager, who can compliment and also reprimand in the right way. Others, particularly the managers themselves, claim that they have to retain a certain distance to preserve their authority.

Without saying more on the subject, take this test and see how you feel about this.

┌─ Test ─

1. Think of three coworkers.
   (a) Do you know all their spouses' or
       companions' names?   Yes ☐   No ☐
   (b) Have you ever been to their homes?   Yes ☐   No ☐
   (c) Have you invited one or more to your
       home?   Yes ☐   No ☐
   (d) How much do you know about their
       backgrounds? (for instance, where they
       were born?)   Little ☐   Much ☐   A few facts ☐

   (Continued)

2. In regard to your coworkers, would you like to:
   (*a*) Meet more often socially. (If you select this one, list 1, 2, 3, or more coworkers this applies to.) ☐
   (*b*) See only at workplace. ☐
   (*c*) Xmas parties, etc. are enough. ☐
   (*d*) Tell them more about yourself. (If you select this one, list 1, 2, 3, or more coworkers this applies to.) ☐

3. A valuable coworker just gave notice. How would you most likely feel:
   (*a*) Now I'll have to retrain someone else. ☐
   (*b*) I'll miss that person's good nature. ☐
   (*c*) Perhaps I was lacking something as a supervisor. ☐
   (*d*) No big deal. ☐

4. How do you feel when your coworkers come to you with their personal problems?
   (*a*) I would rather not be involved. ☐
   (*b*) I try to help if I can. ☐
   (*c*) I am not a professional; they would be better off to see one. ☐
   (*d*) It might interfere with work discipline. ☐

5. A coworker comes to your office complaining about a colleague. What do you do?
   (*a*) I tell them both to settle the dispute themselves. ☐
   (*b*) I call them both to my office and listen carefully to both sides. ☐
   (*c*) I ask someone else to talk to one first and report back to me. ☐
   (*d*) I tell one to wait a while and see whether things get better. ☐

Scoring and Interpretation

1. (*a*) Yes = 4 (*b*) Yes = 4 (*c*) Yes = 4 (*d*) Little = 2
   No = 1   No = 1   No = 1   A few facts = 3
                                    Much = 4

2. (a) 1 = 2   (*b*) = 1   (*c*) = 1   (*d*) 1 = 2
   2 = 3   2 = 3
   3 or more = 4   3 or more = 4

3. (*a*) = 2   4. (*a*) = 1   5. (*a*) = 1
   (*b*) = 3   (*b*) = 4   (*b*) = 4
   (*c*) = 4   (*c*) = 3   (*c*) = 3
   (*d*) = 1   (*d*) = 2   (*d*) = 2

Compute your scores according to the values given in the above key.

> If you are a good communicator and interested in your colleagues, your score is between 26 and 32.
>
> You take a more aloof attitude and try to separate involvement from business attitudes if you score between 18 and 25.
>
> A low score, 9 to 17, describes you as uninterested in the private lives of your associates.

We conducted an experiment for the American Medical Association. Patients were encouraged to call their physicians by first names. The older doctors felt that this intimacy would upset the professional relationship. They agreed to cooperate by using the excuse of participating in a scientific experiment. To their surprise, many felt that they had not lost authority, but instead had achieved a better, more honest understanding based on mutual respect. Much depends, of course, on the circumstances. Personal relations are usually better and more helpful than impersonal ones.

However, in some circumstances it is better not to be involved in the personal affairs of coworkers. For example, when there are non-work-related conflicts among members of your staff, it is usually better to keep your distance. Otherwise, you risk being accused of bias. In such a case, the less you know, the better your chances for objectivity.

On the other hand, a productive coworker may suddenly slow down and not perform as well as before. Nothing obvious seems to be wrong. Your questions do not elicit satisfying answers, but you happen to know from previous discussions that there is a problem in the marriage. This acquired knowledge can help you understand the reason for loss of productivity.

The possibilities for miscommunication between managers and employees are great. The fault may be the manager's lack of interest in the personal lives of coworkers.

HOW GOOD A LISTENER ARE YOU?

When a coworker complains of not being appreciated, often what is meant is that no one is listening. Achievements, ideas, and even mistakes are being ignored. Many of us think that in order to listen, all we need do is bend an ear in the direction of the speaker. We have developed a few tests which indicate your skills as a good listener.

Test

Select the one answer for each question that best expresses your feelings.

1. Try to remember the last time you listened to a presentation or a speech. If you can't, use this test when there is a new opportunity for you to be a listener. Then answer truthfully which applies most to you.
   (*a*) I refuse to waste my time with a boring speaker. ☐
   (*b*) I am pretty good at listening. Even a bore usually has something worthwhile to say. ☐
   (*c*) I try to do something else while I pretend to listen, unless I am really excited about the talk. ☐
   (*d*) I try to summarize what the person really wanted to say. That forces me to pay attention. ☐

2. How would your staff or your boss or even your spouse rate your listening qualifications?
   (*a*) I am a thousand miles away. ☐
   (*b*) I don't listen. I always make people repeat what they've just said. ☐
   (*c*) I appear not to listen, but really I hear every word. ☐
   (*d*) I am very attentive. ☐

3. Someone has a strong accent and is difficult to understand. What are you most likely to do?
   (*a*) Ask the person to repeat. ☐
   (*b*) Stop listening. ☐
   (*c*) Try to catch a few words and figure out the rest. ☐
   (*d*) Listen very carefully—maybe make notes or a record so I can listen again. ☐

4. Someone makes the following statements during a conversation. Which one would you most likely accept?
   (*a*) I am not afraid to speak in public. It is just my bad luck that the few times when I was supposed to get up and address a group I was hoarse. ☐
   (*b*) I think this promotion could not have been given to a nicer person. If I had had to decide myself, that is the person I would have chosen. ☐
   (*c*) I don't really know the answer to that question. I never bothered to think about it. ☐
   (*d*) Can you please explain it in simpler terms? I don't know much about it. ☐

5. Someone speaks in a very low voice. Most likely it means that the person
   (*a*) Wants to be able to cover a mistake. ☐
   (*b*) Is shy. ☐

(c) Has a low voice.   ☐

(d) Is compensating for the loud voices nearby—it forces one to listen closely.   ☐

Scoring and Interpretation

1. $(a)=1$	2. $(a)=1$	3. $(a)=2$	4. $(a)=1$	5. $(a)=3$
$(b)=3$	$(b)=2$	$(b)=1$	$(b)=2$	$(b)=2$
$(c)=2$	$(c)=3$	$(c)=3$	$(c)=3$	$(c)=1$
$(d)=4$	$(d)=4$	$(d)=4$	$(d)=4$	$(d)=4$

Compute your scores according to the values given in the above key.

The highest score is 16 to 20. You pay attention to the obvious points made but also to deeper meanings. You are a good listener.

A score of 10 to 15 indicates an average tendency to show interest in coworkers when they tell you something but also a tendency to avoid wasting your time if you believe the message to be unimportant.

A score of 5 to 9 portrays you as a poor listener. You and your peers would benefit by your training to become a better listener.

As a manager, you should be aware of your skill as a listener. Good listeners are generally people-oriented, a quality which is demanded more these days. Not listening is interpreted, quite correctly, as stating that the person has nothing important to say.

If what you hear is not incorporated into your system of thinking and, if need be, translated into your personal language pattern, then you may passively register the sounds but not really communicate. The person talking expects to be heard and understood and wants confirmation of that, even if it is just an "Aha" or a "Hmmm."

Better yet, reviewing your own interpretation of what you heard is greater proof that you, the listener, established a dialogue with the speaker and understood correctly what was being said. This technique helps dispel misinterpretation and leads to improved communication.

Listening can be learned and improved. Being a good listener can enable you to find out more about your coworkers' wishes, frustrations, and fears. Good listening is important to achieving many other managerial goals as well.

Such training is not difficult if you use some ingenuity.

1. Tape a presentation or a lecture and then try to summarize what you heard.

2. In office meetings, jot down the gist of what is being said while it is recorded on tape. Then compare notes to see whether you heard correctly.

3. Make eye contact. This encourages the speaker to express feelings without inhibitions.

4. Make frequent statements of support and understanding. They need not necessarily be more than "Hmmm" or "I see."

5. Avoid scribbling or doodling while listening to someone. It will be interpreted as a lack of interest or even a personal insult.

6. Ask questions. Interrupt politely with relevant remarks. This helps convince the speaker that you are paying close attention.

Listening is more than an acoustic skill. Real listening involves the ability to digest and react to what you have heard. Even when you are learning a foreign language, listening attentively can speed up the learning process.

When you are trying to understand your coworkers better, listening is most important. Paying close attention to the underlying message can reveal reactions and gripes long before they become harmful to work and productivity.

DO YOU FEEL LIKE AN ALIEN IN YOUR COMPANY?

Each company has a culture of its own. The reason underlying the success of many Japanese companies is the employees' loyalty to the corporation and their interest in quality output. However, it's not merely a question of ethics and morality. People are more loyal if they are in tune with the culture of the corporation.

The following questions do not have right or wrong answers. They help establish the type of relationship that exists between members of a corporate family or culture.

Test

Select the one answer for each question that best expresses your feelings.

1. What would the relationship between you and your company resemble most? Are you the company's . . .

   (a) Son/daughter?   ☐

(*b*) Brother/sister? ☐
(*c*) Cousin/nephew? ☐
(*d*) Father/mother? ☐
(*e*) Uncle/aunt? ☐

2. When you are talking about the company, which degree of feeling (measured almost like temperature) would you use to describe it?
   (*a*) Very warm and comfortable. ☐
   (*b*) Businesslike, interested, but not very excited. ☐
   (*c*) It's quid pro quo; no reason to be overly emotional. ☐
   (*d*) On the cool side. ☐

3. What tool would you have to use if you wanted to change some behavior patterns in your company?
   (*a*) A sledgehammer. ☐
   (*b*) A pneumatic drill. ☐
   (*c*) A plane. ☐
   (*d*) A valve adjuster. ☐
   (*e*) A chisel. ☐

4. Psychological distance from your company can be measured symbolically by a scale. On one end there is you; at the other end, the company. How far away are you? (Put a mark on the line where you think you are.)

   10   9   8   7   6   5   4   3   2   1

   You __|___|___|___|___|___|___|___|___|___ Company

5. You have heard a coworker criticize the corporation. When that person is called to task, a number of explanations are offered. Which impresses you most favorably?
   (*a*) I expected overall strong leadership, but there was none. ☐
   (*b*) I needed a clear delineation of my responsibilities, but nothing was forthcoming. ☐
   (*c*) I was never asked about my ideas. No one seemed interested. ☐
   (*d*) I just wanted to point out the company's shortcomings in the hope that this criticism would be accepted positively and would be helpful. ☐

6. Compare your own tempo, melody, or style with that of your company. (Check a letter for you and a letter for the company and then join them.)

I am like		*Company is like*
(*a*)	Waltz	(*a*)
(*b*)	March	(*b*)
(*c*)	Tango	(*c*)
(*d*)	Jazz	(*d*)

Scoring and Interpretation

1. $(a) = 5$ 2. $(a) = 4$ 3. $(a) = 2$
    $(b) = 4$ $(b) = 3$ $(b) = 1$
    $(c) = 1$ $(c) = 2$ $(c) = 4$
    $(d) = 3$ $(d) = 1$ $(d) = 5$
    $(e) = 2$ $(e) = 3$

4. The distance 1 gets a score of 5; distance 2 = 4; distance 3 = 3; distance 4 = 2; distance 5 or more = 1.

5. $(a) = 2$ 6. $(a)–(a) = 4$ $(b)–(b) = 4$ $(c)–(c) = 4$ $(d)–(d) = 4$
   $(b) = 1$ $(a)–(b) = 3$ $(b)–(a) = 3$ $(c)–(b) = 1$ $(d)–(b) = 2$
   $(c) = 3$ $(a)–(c) = 2$ $(b)–(d) = 2$ $(c)–(a) = 2$ $(d)–(a) = 1$
   $(d) = 4$ $(a)–(d) = 1$ $(b)–(c) = 1$ $(c)–(d) = 3$ $(d)–(c) = 3$

Compute your scores according to the values given in the above key.

The highest score is 27. A score from 18 to 27 indicates that you fit very well into the culture of your company. You speak the same psychological language.

A score of 12 to 17 shows a partial feeling of being at home. The distance may be due to not feeling a warm enough relationship or difficulty in changing your company without the use of a sledgehammer.

A score of 7 to 11 reveals maladjustment in one or more areas.

The first step is to make the correct diagnosis. The second step is to change either the attitude of the employee or, if this is impossible, that of the company. They don't have to be identical. A symphony consists of various passages, each one different, but adding up to a harmonious whole.

Anthropologists talk about matriarchal or patriarchal societies. A company can be organized in hierarchical fashion with a strong parent figure at the top or can consist of equal cells and circles, cooperating with one another. A company can be hypocritical, contradictory, competitive, or loving. It is easy to feel comfortable in a culture where the rituals and customs are known. Often U.S. managers abroad experience an unexpected rebuff when they encounter customs contrary to theirs. It can be trivial, but it makes them feel like strangers.

Takeo Doi, a Japanese author, in a book entitled *The Anatomy of Dependence*, tells of an uncomfortable experience.[1] He had been invited

---

[1] Takeo Doi, *The Anatomy of Dependence*, Kodansha International Ltd., Tokyo, 1971, pp. 11–12.

by a U.S. business associate to dinner. He was asked what he wanted to drink. He explained his reaction: "It is part of a Japanese host's politeness not to confront the guest with such decisions. He, the host, should know what his guest's preferences are."

Managing a company and its staff effectively necessitates an awareness of basic cultural labels. Very often, the manager's first job is to find out whether a corporation has a clear-cut philosophy or credo. The first acculturation should take place during hiring of new staff; i.e., managers should help them feel at home and yet preserve their identity. In fact, identity crises are often the cause of malfunctioning within a well-balanced organization.

The reason for firing someone is usually cited as incompatibility. Employees, like ambassadors in a foreign land, can't adapt to the strange corporate environment. Cultures and credos change with years, just as the staff does. Workers getting older and bored with the routine nature of the work can create disharmony.

It is a good idea to try to crystallize a company's credo and condense it to an understandable form. Describe the philosophy to applicants; this can help prevent hiring of the wrong people. In the same way, within a company, pointing out discrepancies between professed managerial goals and real ones can avert disappointments and frustration.

WHO NEEDS APPLAUSE?

Most personal success is based in good measure on self-assurance. However, I was told the reason for my success was my insecurity, which enabled me to develop better insight into other people's attitudes. Actors, even the most successful ones, admit to having the jitters before a stage appearance. Much depends on the degree of compensation. Was Hitler secure or insecure? He probably doubted himself but found he could overcompensate by playing the fanatic.

When you are hiring or promoting a coworker, how deep should you probe his or her self-assurance? Unfortunately, we tend to pigeonhole people into superficial categories. In this test, we tried to get to the core of self-appreciation.

Test

1. List as many of your good and bad qualities as you can think of. Then ask yourself how friends or acquaintances would fill out the list

(Continued)

---

of your best and worst qualities. (By qualities we mean being loving, unloving, resentful, reliable, intelligent, considerate, friendly, communicative, reasonable, stubborn, etc.) Do not use a checklist. It is important to know which qualities you pick spontaneously.

Me		Friends	
Good	Bad	Good	Bad

2. During an office party X makes a very awkward remark which is audible to everyone: "You certainly can't hold a job!" What would be the most likely reaction of most of the other people?
   (a) That's typical of X, always caught with a foot in the mouth. ☐
   (b) There must be a more subtle way of putting that. ☐
   (c) What a person! Certainly not a hypocrite! ☐
   (d) That's none of X's business. ☐

3. List the qualities in yourself that you need to improve. How many are there?
   (a) Four to five. ☐
   (b) None. ☐
   (c) Almost everything. ☐
   (d) A lot. ☐

4. Try to draw a so-called sociogram. Put down your various friends, collaborators, and acquaintances on a sort of map. Then connect the various people with lines. When the relationship is a one-sided one, draw an arrow with the arrowhead either from you to the other person or the other way around. If the relationship is mutual, put an arrowhead on both ends. You can get an even more complete picture if you indicate closeness of the relationship by using lines of various thicknesses. For example, consider the sample at the top of page 135.

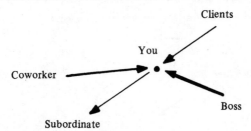

You get a graphic illustration of how popular you are, how many relationships you have, and how one-sided or mutual your relationships are. Now draw a sociogram for yourself:

5. How would you rate yourself as far as emotional warmth (plus) or coolness (minus) toward your coworkers is concerned?

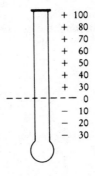

6. You meet a new colleague for the first time. You are not sure what impression you made. When you meet again, do you feel that the colleague is likely to
(a) Have an improved impression of you.   ☐

(Continued)

(b) Have the same impression of you as before. ☐

(c) Have a worse impression of you. ☐

Scoring and Interpretation

1. If you listed more bad qualities than good, give yourself a 4. You are honest and self-assured. If you assigned more good qualities than bad ones to yourself, you seem self-assured but are less likely to be so. We would grant you a score of 3.

   If you claim that your friends list more bad qualities than good about you, we would interpret this as lack of self-assurance and assign a score of 2.

   On the other hand, if more good qualities are mentioned by your acquaintances or colleagues than you listed for yourself, we would give you a score of 4. You are, despite other doubts, quite self-assured.

   The type of qualities chosen is also important. (Usually we found more cognitive intellectual ones among the positive qualities and more emotional qualities among the negative ones.)

2. (a) = 1   3. (a) = 2
   (b) = 3   (b) = 1
   (c) = 4   (c) = 3
   (d) = 2   (d) = 4

4. The more two-way arrows you can sketch in, the better. Give yourself a 4 if you have more than four two-way arrows. For each arrow less or one-sided arrow, deduct 1 point. This test has most value as a diagram visualizing your contacts with your coworkers. Negative scores are possible.

5. Up to 30 = 1   6. (a) = 3
      30–50 = 2   (b) = 2
      50–70 = 3   (c) = 1
   above 70 = 4

Compute your scores according to the values given in the above key.

The total best score is 15 to 23. You are quite sure of yourself and accept others' negative opinions of you.

A score of 10 to 14, depending on its composition, may have been influenced by a certain coolness or lack of contact with coworkers. That is, more than 50 percent in our pretest felt that their colleagues would have an improved impression after two additional meetings.

We gave a positive score even if you listed bad qualities about yourself, or if your colleague listed them, because it shows a readiness to see yourself realistically.

A score of 6 to 9 is a poor sign—if it relates to a lack of readiness to improve yourself.

In testing or hiring an applicant, a willingness to grow should be considered particularly important. The person you hire should be judged by a readiness to grow and to develop regardless of age. People who are at a standstill as far as their personal qualities are concerned often find themselves on a dead-end street as far as their professional aspects are concerned.

Your company should offer training courses and seminars for the development of new products and have a research and development department for psychological and occupational qualities. Being too self-assured may hide weakness. Equally, being too self-deprecating may be a way of trying to disarm others and thwart criticism.

Repeating and emphasizing one's "stupidity" can be a particularly dangerous mask. An aggressive person pretending to be overaccommodating can mislead you. Proper motivation involves being immune to the false flatterer, not being taken in by the "helpless" person, winking at the worrywart, and standing up to the bully.

HOW CRYPTIC ARE YOU?

One of the most frequent complaints of employees is that they are not appreciated or understood. "Nobody listens to me. I don't mean anything to this organization." Does this sound familiar?

To understand these complaints and help you become a better manager and communicator, we have tried to discover what communication really involves. One error is to consider it as a one-way street. A closer look will show that true communication is a dialogue. It's not enough to bark an order and assume you have communicated your desire correctly. You should understand what happens in the mind of the recipient. Often the message is not understood in the way you intended.

For example, you ask me why I have a blue sweater. The word *why* contains several pitfalls. Did you mean what made me buy it? Did you mean who persuaded me to buy it? Did you simply want to know why I chose blue rather than another color? Because the question is too vague, the answer is meaningless. In business, accurate communication goes hand in hand with being a good leader or administrator.

An excellent way to make sure your instructions have been fully understood is to ask your coworker to explain the assignment to you again. Another safeguard would be to ask your coworker how to best execute the request. Using a so-called open-ended form of interviewing, psychoanalysts often repeat the answer they have just heard to determine whether they have correctly interpreted what was said.

Often explanations are completely unclear. Here are some proven suggestions for improving communication.

1. Go through your instructions with the person receiving them. Cover each step clearly, and avoid broad, general commands.

2. Give an example by stating, "This is how I might go about it."

3. Make it a joint project by saying, "Let's start it together; then you can continue. If you need help, call me."

4. Ask another, more experienced, person to help explain further.

5. Don't give directions in a bossy way. Allow and encourage employees to ask questions. They are often intimidated.

6. Don't expect people to read your mind. Always assume there might be a gap in understanding.

Listening and really grasping or integrating a statement are two different things. You can listen to a lecture and take notes but still not understand what was said. If you are listening to a management training course, it is helpful to summarize what the speaker has conveyed. You may discover that you have not paid attention or have failed to grasp the gist of the lecture.

If you are the lecturer, make sure your audience is listening and, even more important, that they understand what you are saying. Interrupt your talk every so often to ask for a reaction. Ask them to give you parallel examples of what you have mentioned. Or challenge them by asking how they would apply what they've just heard to their own businesses.

One danger is to address a passive audience and feel happy because they are scribbling away, taking notes. Unfortunately, I once noticed, while applying a sequence of numbers to certain points, that the audience was more concerned with the order of the points than with their meaning. So it is, too, with managers. Do your coworkers follow your instructions by rote, or do they understand the ultimate goal? Which is better? Which promotes interest and cooperation? Which lessens resentment and engenders self-assurance and self-worth?

Subconscious Understanding

Most physicians know that even an unimportant statement often causes a patient anxiety. The same is true in an organization where someone has the power to reprimand or compliment. A rather innocuous remark is often misinterpreted. There are many examples where top executives failed to perceive the negativity in a remark. Someone saying "This promotion could not have happened to a nicer person" may sound harmless. But if that person repeats it several times, it can become a denial of the compliment. In many training courses, the executives in charge have been told to compliment their employees as often as possible, certainly when it is deserved. If done too often, though, it becomes perfunctory and the compliment loses its real meaning.

An important part of communication is guessing what is happening in the mind of the dialogue partner. Psychoanalysts are trained to put a patient at ease by stating that it is normal to feel awkward, and want to walk out. Doing this creates an affinity and puts the client at ease almost immediately.

The "aha" experience is another important element of communication. We can influence others by relying on their instincts. This applies not only to animals but also to human behavior. We can produce better results by training through a punishment-reward system. But the real form of influence (and the most human aspect of learning) is seen when we create an "aha" experience. When, on a deeper level of perception, we notice some kind of a "click," a response and awareness of recognition. What we are trying to communicate has been integrated and has been learned.

Psychodrama is another educational method. It was originally developed by Dr. J.L. Moreno, a Viennese psychiatrist who wanted to resolve interpersonal conflicts. He asked professional actors to play the roles of husband, wife, and children, acting out on stage real-life situations. In this fashion, the family members could see themselves in a new dynamic reality and understand the nature of their conflicts. Similar techniques can be used in managerial situations to facilitate better communication between adversaries and/or coworkers in general.

Above all, top managers must listen—not just with their ears but with their eyes and hearts as well.

CONCLUSION

The tests in this book do not so much evaluate the present and potential abilities of a top manager as they help the reader to gain insight into the main function of good management—assuming a leadership role that requires expertise, skill, and knowledge in the field of operation.

Management, however, is more an art than a science. We all have our very individual approaches to handling the short- and long-range questions, problems, dilemmas, and decisions which are as varied in professional arenas as in our personal lives. Our skills are used in a different way in different situations and at different periods in our careers.

There is no scientific way of proving that one style of directing and convincing coworkers produces better results than another. What is fairly certain, however, is that playing phoney roles that do not fit us makes us uneasy with ourselves and with our peers.

Good management is a total philosophy overriding the individual functions and tests of this or other books. Unless we have such a philosophy and act according to our deeper beliefs, learned skills will not be very helpful.

This book tries to offer guidance in developing an inventory of possible managerial attitudes and techniques, permitting comparison with executives in similar situations. How an individual manager rates himself or herself is the real test of managerial abilities. It is up to each person to develop and sharpen these tools and adapt them to the specific lifestyle and field of operation, remembering always that human relations and communication remain at the base of every successful business enterprise.

BIBLIOGRAPHY

Adizes, Ichak: *How to Solve the Mismanagement Crisis*, Adizes Institute, Santa Monica, California, 1983.
Cialdini, Robert B.: *Influence*, Morrow, New York, 1984.
Didato, Salvatore V.: *Psychotechniques*, Methuen, New York, 1980.
Drucker, Peter F.: *Managing in Turbulent Times*, Harper & Row, New York, 1980.
Esfandiary, F. M.: *Optimism One*, Norton, New York, 1970.
Furst, Sconey: *Business Decisions*, Random House, New York, 1964.
Lunding, Franklin J.: *Sharing a Business*, Updegraff Press, Munich, Germany, 1951.
Marrow, Alfred J., Bowers, David G., Seashore Stanley E.,: *Management by Participation*, Harper & Row, New York, 1967.
Roper, Elmo: *You and Your Leaders*, Morrow, New York, 1957.
Uris, Auren: *Mastery of Managements*, Dow Jones-Irwin, Homewood, Illinois, 1968.
Vough, Clair F.: *Tapping the Human Resource*, Amacom, New York, 1975.

INDEX

About the Author

Ernest Dichter is professor of management, Long Island University, and president of an international management and motivational research company. During his career he has served as a consultant to some of the largest international firms and advertising agencies, including General Motors, AT&T, CBS, Philip Morris, Johnson & Johnson, Lufthansa, The New York Times, Young and Rubicam, Leo Burnett, and Foot Cone & Belding.

Ernest Dichter originated the concept of motivational research—the application of modern psychological techniques to management, advertising, communications, and politics—and many of his published works have become standards of the marketing literature. Among his books are *Handbook of Consumer Motivation, Motivating Human Behavior, The Naked Manager, The Strategy of Desire,* and his autobiography, *Getting Motivated.* He is also the author of hundreds of articles in both professional and popular magazines, and he is in wide demand as a public speaker. In 1983 he was elected a member of the hall of fame of the Market Research Council.